Unleashing Your

Inner Witch

Unleashing Your Inner Witch

An Introductory Guide for New Witches

DELIA RAVEN BLACK

Kailua-Kona, HI

Paperback ISBN: 979-8-9904445-0-8

First Edition, 2024.

Dedicated to my husband, Matthew, for encouraging me to put my witchy knowledge and teachings into writing, to my parents and teachers along the way for your encouragement and wisdom, and to you, my readers, for your curiosity and courage to unleash the inner witch waiting inside of you.

Table of Contents

Conjuring Knowledge: Expanding What You Know Beyond Beginner

Introduction

Welcome, Seeker.

Within these pages, you will find a sacred space of endless possibilities.

It is here that I extend an invitation to new witches to a path of self-discovery, a map of the vast landscape of witchcraft, and a manual for casting spells that harmonize with your soul.

Whether you're taking your first steps on the magical path or seeking to deepen your understanding, this guide will be your companion throughout your journey of discovery. *Unleashing Your Inner Witch* serves as a mentor for the curious and those who seek knowledge, and as a companion for those who are ready to unfurl their wings in the world of witchcraft. As you eagerly seek to learn the craft, may these pages serve as a comforting voice sharing its secrets with you.

Imagine this book is a magical doorway that invites you to step through and discover the many different landscapes that witchcraft has to offer. You are about to go on an adventure that will reveal the secrets of seven different types of this wonderful craft. Whether you are drawn to the rhythmic pull of the moon, the rigid form of tradition, or the unpredictability of chaos, you have chosen to embrace your curiosity. As you step onto the mystical path of exploration, know that the choices you make and the paths you traverse are as unique as you. The capacity to tune into your intuition—a guide that predates recorded history—and to follow your natural curiosity are two of the most crucial skills for a witch to have.

Witchcraft is as diverse as the stars in the night sky, and within these pages you'll find a map guiding you to your place among them. Each type of witchcraft is a constellation, waiting for you to connect the dots that resonate with your spirit.

As you start down this road, imagine each word as a stepping stone, guiding you toward the inner sanctum where your true self resides. This is more than a manual—it is a companion on your journey of self-exploration, a mirror reflecting the beauty and strength that lie within you.

Prepare to travel through the sacred meadows of Wicca, study and practice the heart of Traditional Witchcraft, venture through the garden paths of Green Magic, and linger by the hearth with Kitchen Witches.

Let the glow of these words continue to illuminate your path as you traverse boundaries and explore the in-between spaces with the Hedge Witch and experience the dance of unpredictability and liberation of Chaos Magick, where the unexpected sparks creativity.

Finally, you will conclude your exploration with Eclectic Witchcraft, which weaves together the threads of the various rich traditions covered in this guide into a brilliant tapestry.

Setting Your Intention

Before we plunge into the practical aspects of witchcraft, I invite you to take a moment to set your intention. In the quiet of your own space, let your heart speak. What draws you to the craft? Is it the allure of ancient wisdom, the desire for personal empowerment, or an unspoken connection to the mystical forces that surround us?

Write your thoughts, dreams, and desires in the margins of these pages, or begin a journal—your very own Book of Shadows, if you will. Let them be the ink that weaves your story into the fabric of this magical journey.

When you are ready, set your intention.

Spell for Inner Power

What you will need:

- A place of peace and quiet
- A single sheet of paper
- A pen
- A small wooden box (optional)

Incantation

In this quiet space, I begin,

to unearth the power that lies within.

With paper and pen, my journey starts,

to discover the magic that lies within my heart.

Instructions

1. Find a place that is safe, quiet, and comfortable.

2. Take a few deep breaths to center yourself.

3. On the piece of paper, write down your intention to explore your inner power and discover your unique magic. It can be a simple statement: "I discover." Or, you can simply write down the incantation above (as you learn about witchcraft and the style that suits you best, you may set your intention again with the new knowledge that you have).

4. When you are writing, pay attention to the words and the energy that is held within them. The point is to feel it and believe it.

5. Fold the paper toward you, first in half, then again. Folding it toward yourself invites the magic and intention in, binding it to you.

6. As you fold, recite the incantation above.

7. Keep the paper as a reminder of your commitment to self-discovery. Store it in your small wooden box. You can always return to it and reread it whenever you need to.

Embracing the Unknown

In the art of witchcraft, we embrace the unknown, the shadows that dance on the periphery of our understanding of the world. Let this book be your lantern in the dark—it does not cast out those shadows, but illuminates them and brings out the beauty in them. It is a guide that encourages you to tread lightly, to explore, and to question—because it is in the darkness that we discover our own light, and it is in the questions that we find the answers.

As you embark on this sacred journey, may the wisdom of the ages and the murmurs of the wisest among you accompany you. *Unleashing Your Inner Witch* is a call to embrace your inner witch and find wonder in the mundane.

This book is the key that will allow you to unlock the treasure trove of your own personal magic. Each chapter serves as a guidepost, providing information about the seven types of witchcraft as well as the numerous ways in which you can infuse your craft with your own personal intention.

As you turn these pages, may you experience the warmth of a community that extends beyond the boundaries of time and space; may you feel the bonds of sisterhood and brotherhood among the witches who came before.

And so you hold a manual for weaving spells that are not only potent but intimately tied to who you are. These spells are not mere words; they are the echoes of your intentions, the whispers of your desires, and the harmonies of your innermost self.

Discover the art of infusing your magic with a personal touch, crafting spells that resonate not only with universal energies but also with the very essence of your being.

Begin your journey through this book with Part I, where the foundational aspects of witchcraft await your exploration, offering essential insights to deepen your understanding of the craft, culminating in a quiz to help you identify your witchcraft type in Chapter 3.

Part II is dedicated to chapters for each of the seven types of witchcraft covered in this book, offering a brief overview, guidance on setting up your space, and spells tailored to each type. If you are ever in doubt, the Glossary is there to define terms and briefly explain the uses of specific items, while the "Witchy Products" page conveniently links you to valuable resources for your spells.

Whether you navigate Part II sequentially or intuitively, each chapter unveils its own unique approach, guiding you on your path of discovery. Regardless of your approach, be sure to read the Conclusion, where the threads of wisdom come together.

As you unearth your inner witch and traverse the seven paths calling to you, open your heart, embrace the magic within, and allow the words on these pages to be your guiding light.

Blessed be.

Part I:

Embracing the Witch Within–
A Personal Journey

Chapter 1:

The Mystical Evolution of Witchcraft

Before we embark on this journey together, let's pause and take a breath. It is so important to understand the histories and trace the steps of those mages who practiced before us. Our journey begins not just with spells and potions but with a reverence for the roots that anchor our craft, connecting us to the wisdom of those who came before.

So, dear Seeker, before we kindle the first flame, let us unfurl the parchment of our ancient histories and walk the path of our ancestors.

Over the centuries, the practice of witchcraft—a complex web of beliefs and practices drawn from all over the world—has taken on countless forms.

The fascinating evolution of witchcraft into what it is today is truly remarkable. During this brief historical exploration, we will discover its presence and variation across eras and witness the kaleidoscope of cultures that have shaped its essence.

Ancient Roots

For humans, witchcraft evolved from an early desire for deep and personal communion with nature—a desire to connect with and understand the world around us. From the Sumerians to the Egyptians and beyond, all ancient cultures had profound respect for practitioners of the mystical arts. Early practitioners were regarded as wise folk, healers, and guardians of sacred mysteries. These magicians sprouted the seeds for our ancient roots.

Witchcraft was more than just a set of esoteric rites; it was a collection of intricate rituals that echoed the very heartbeat of the Earth. In these ancient civilizations, it was an integral part of daily life that included seeing into the future, making elixirs from herbs, and communicating with other worlds. Practitioners were esteemed for their intricate knowledge, as they held the keys to healing, divination, and understanding the unseen forces that shaped the world.

Our predecessors were loved for their connection with the world—and at a time when we needed to understand the world most. We were but infants in the grand cosmological timeline, and, like babes, we needed the guidance of gods and greater powers so we could forge our paths.

These ancient witches had an unspoken but profound connection with the elements and guarded important secrets. Through elaborate rituals, they attempted to harmonize themselves with the unseen powers that were present in every part of their lives. These rituals were not mere performances; they were conduits through which the practitioners could navigate the intricate dance between the tangible and the ethereal, seeking wisdom, balance, and a profound connection to the elemental forces that sculpted the very fabric of their reality so they could share the voice of the gods with mortal men and women.

In this dance with the unseen, those ancient witches wove a tapestry of knowledge, spirituality, and harmony that echoed through the ages, leaving an indelible mark on the evolving narrative of our craft.

A Medieval Shadow

Unfortunately, not all remained in awe of our power.

Soon enough, the branches that had grown and blossomed across continents were violently cut back.

The dark shadow of the Middle Ages descended upon the practice of witchcraft in the Western world, which caused a ripple effect across the globe. In an age where societal structures underwent seismic shifts, so too did perceptions of the craft. No longer revered as benevolent caretakers of ancient wisdom, witches and diviners found themselves ensnared in insidious webs of fear and superstition.

Collectively, the once-respected practitioners—wise women who had been pillars of their communities and those who held a profound connection to the rhythms of nature—now became figures to be sought out and destroyed. The shift in societal norms and religious fervor birthed an era where the mystical became menacing and those with knowledge of herbs, healing, and the unseen were viewed with suspicion and hate.

Witch hunts, which were fueled by a potent cocktail of religious zealotry and societal paranoia, descended upon the Western world, echoing across civilizations and starting the dark chapter that has left an indelible mark on the histories of our craft. With their perverted understandings of the supernatural, inquisitors went in search of individuals who were suspected of having associations with evil forces.

The belief that witches were brokering deals in exchange for these gifts—and, at that, brokering deals with the devil of the Christian religion—was the spark that lit the fires of the Salem witch trials in America. In Europe and Salem, even women who simply stood up to powerful men were put to death or accused of witchcraft during the witch trials. Women, men, and even children who behaved in ways that most people thought were strange or not like them were accused of witchcraft. This included healers and women who spoke their minds without fear—a perfect catalyst for the coming darkness.

The trials gave rise to the idea that witchcraft, in its many manifestations—including the ability to stand in your power, heal with herbs, or produce an outcome that people could not explain—should be seen as evil.

Witchcraft, in its very essence, became synonymous with heresy, and those who were accused of practicing it faced dire consequences. Our practices, rooted in ancient teachings and handed down through generations, were grossly misunderstood and condemned. Everything we knew was torn asunder.

Yet, within this darkness, the resilient spirit of the craft endured, awaiting the dawn of a new era.

Renaissance Revival

A profound change in the intellectual landscape occurred as a result of the Renaissance, ushering in new ideas and new beliefs. Visionaries such as Agrippa and Dee sought to reconcile magic with the emerging currents of scientific thought. Magic and science were halves of the same whole. While Dee had a hand in developing alchemy and deciphering Enochian, the language of angels (a personal favorite language of mine), Agrippa's work had a significant impact on the development of magic and occultism. His ideas contributed to the intellectual climate of the Renaissance, where there was a revival of interest in Hermeticism (see the Glossary) and other mystical traditions.

During the Renaissance, the ancient art of magic found renewed expression in the still-evolving worldviews of the time. This marked the beginning of a period of transformation.

Renaissance thinkers embarked on a quest to harmonize the seemingly disparate worlds of magic and science, trying to unite and shed light on the craft that had been exiled to the darkest reaches of human memory.

Grimoires—collections of esoteric knowledge—flourished and served as a guide for those who were eager to investigate the boundaries between the natural and the supernatural. The writings of Agrippa and Dee, among others, became stars on this celestial map, guiding souls through the uncharted territories of the mystical and magical arts. Our witchy ancestors found themselves filled with renewed hope.

The traditional arts of magic, once relegated to the fringes of societal understanding, now stood side by side with the burgeoning scientific thought. The intellectual alchemy of magic and science forged a path for Seekers, and grimoires became guiding stars in the celestial expanse of the arcane. It was an era when the boundaries of human knowledge expanded and the mystical arts found new expressions in the evolving worldviews of the time. Modern witches still carry the spirit of that revolutionary age in their minds.

However, yet again, a period of unrest was on the horizon—a continuous war between witches and those who did not understand our craft.

An Enlightened Transition

With the Age of Enlightenment came a resurgence of skepticism toward the mystical and, with it, a new-found reasoning that threatened to extinguish witchcraft once and for all.

The magic that had been woven into the fabric of human history was confronted with a formidable challenge in the Enlightenment, which was characterized by an intellectual fervor that championed scientific inquiry and critical thinking. Ancient practices were relegated to the realms of superstition and folklore as a result of popular skepticism, which threatened to extinguish the mystical flames that were ablaze. Witchcraft, which was once a highly regarded practice, was now once again relegated to the shadows of society.

Yet, hidden communities devoted to esoteric practices and knowledge persisted despite this. In order to protect the ancient arts from the prying eyes of a rationalistic world, these clandestine gatherings became safe havens for those individuals who were interested in preserving them. Within these secret societies that held onto the mysteries of witchcraft, practitioners kept the dim embers of alchemy, astrology, and mysticism lit while simultaneously shielding them from the scrutiny of the Enlightenment.

Throughout history, alchemists, astrologists, and mystics have persisted as covert torchbearers, quietly preserving the ancient wisdom that would one day inspire a resurgence of magical exploration.

Our roots ran deep, steadying our resolve, and our hope carried us through the darkest of times, to the very moment where our power could no longer be snuffed like a candle in a storm.

Modern Alchemy

The rebirth came with freedom of information.

There was a resurgence of interest in witchcraft in the 20th century, thanks to prominent figures like Gerald Gardner and Doreen Valiente, who helped people rediscover the ancient arts. Again, we stepped out of the shadows to teach those willing to learn of our practices, and this time our hope and faith were well-founded.

This period saw the birth of Wicca, a modern interpretation deeply rooted in age-old traditions. Wicca became the cornerstone, laying the foundation for a diverse array of paths by focusing on nature and being steeped in ritual. These contemporary paths include Traditional, Eclectic, Solitary, and more. In the midst of this period of profound transformation, the modern witch, who is sensitive to the reverberations of traditional practices, emerged as a protector of ancient knowledge in a world that is undergoing rapid transformation.

While still under scrutiny from major world religions like Christianity, we stood bold and proud.

Gardner and Valiente, who had a desire to revive the mystical arts, contributed significantly to the rekindling of our practices. Working together, they revived long-lost rituals and introduced new ideas that would shape modern witchcraft.

Wicca's sphere of influence reached far beyond its humble beginnings. It became a catalyst, inspiring diverse paths within the broader umbrella of modern witchcraft. The adaptable structure that Wicca offered was a place where Traditional covens, solitary Eclectic practitioners, and individuals who were forging their own unique individual paths found resonance.

15

As a result, modern witches were not limited by a single definition; rather, they discovered a sense of belonging in mutual respect for knowledge of the past—knowledge shared by our ancestors—and a heart of hope for a bright future.

As the world went through a period of rapid change and technological advancement, we emerged as protectors of the knowledge that had been preserved and passed down for generations. Grimoires became a witch's Book of Shadows. And the Book of Shadows became not only a guide for rituals but also a testament to the enduring legacy of witches who had the courage to defy each year of persecution and dance with the mystical in a world that was constantly changing.

Technological Transitions

At this point in time, magic has undergone a profound transformation, having been forged in the fires and come through the other side, changed—but stronger. Persecuted and regaled to the darkest shadows of time, our kind were hunted to near extinction and yet continuously found new footholds.

No longer are we relegated to the dark corners of society; no longer are we forced to shutter our lanterns of light and power, for we have entered the age of technology.

While there are still those who prefer the tangibility of writing with ink on paper, witches who prefer to keep a close physical connection with their craft and community, we have, mostly, shifted into the online realm, and our Book of Shadows is now a digital grimoire.

The village square has been replaced by social media platforms and online communities where practitioners share their insights, spells, and support with one another. An important new chapter in the ongoing story of witchcraft has been written as a result of the convergence of ancient knowledge and cutting-edge technology. Covens, once bound by physical proximity, now traverse and expand within virtual spaces, where sacred groves coalesce with the light of virtual worlds.

From Instagram to TikTok, practitioners share snippets of their craft—snapshots of their daily lives—showcasing rituals, spells, and practices, giving and seeking advice. Online communities offer a space for discourse, support, and the exchange of magical knowledge, creating a vibrant tapestry of digital camaraderie. If you're more comfortable staying out of the online spotlight (which is a perfectly valid choice), you can still participate if you so desire by using a pseudonym or simply listening and learning from others. Of course, another option is to stay offline entirely, should you feel the need.

No matter if you choose to participate in this online world or not, the transition symbolizes not just a change in medium but the adaptability and steadfast endurance of our age-old craft in the face of change.

Our magical ancestors are openly and proudly being called upon yet again.

A Tapestry Unfolding

Here we are in an ever-evolving modern era, and the web of magic is still being spun. Every witch has their own unique role to play in the history of witchcraft, as we are all spellcasters and weavers of magic. We are the storytellers of our craft, the future ancestors our descendants will draw their power from, and it is humbling.

The lessons of the ancients, the trials of the medieval, the revival of the Renaissance, the transitions of the Enlightenment, and the modern alchemy of the 20th and 21st centuries—these all are threads in this rich narrative. As the pages turn, the story beckons those of us who are brave enough to listen, inviting us to become a part of the ongoing tale of witchcraft and its secrets that transcend time.

You, dear Seeker, are part of this new transition. Your magic will become part of future histories and shape the landscape of witchcraft—if only you dare.

Chapter 2:

Understanding the Power Within You and How to Harness the Elements

Today you stand at the precipice of witchcraft, ready to carve your own path, while the histories of the craft continue to be written, connecting ancient witches to your modern magic. Embrace your role in this unfolding story, for your journey adds a unique touch to the creation of magic.

Within this chapter, you will find the guidance you need to move toward growth, self-actualization, and empowerment. Together, we will uncover the true abilities that reside within you as we delve into the unknown and carefully untangle the links that bind you to your magical nature.

Embarking on the Inner Odyssey

In order to conquer the outside world, we must first go within and tap into our own hidden strength. You will be able to discover the reservoirs of energy that are waiting for your command by engaging in self-reflection, practicing meditation, and receiving the gentle caress of ancient wisdom. In order to lay the groundwork for a harmonious relationship with the elements, the journey inward is essential.

This introspective journey is not just a normal step in your journey; it is a pivotal prelude to mastering the external forces that intertwine with your magical power.

Meditation as the Gateway

Taking the time to reflect and meditate is not a detour but the very foundation upon which your connection to the elements is built. The recognition, embrace, and exploration of your inner power lay the groundwork for a magical practice that resonates with authenticity and strength.

Meditation serves as the gateway to the inner realms. As you dive into the practice, you will discover a way to escape the noise of the outside world and explore the depths of your own mind. The stillness will help you connect with your innermost self, where your boundless, untapped energy source resides.

To make things easier for you, I have included a short meditation ritual to set you on your path.

Self-Reflection Meditation

1. Get yourself to a peaceful, comfy spot where you will not be interrupted. Set the mood for relaxation by turning down the lights or lighting a candle. Or, if you feel drawn to do so, have a seat outside!

2. Express your intention of engaging in self-reflection clearly.

It might be a specific question you have or just a general yearning for more understanding in some part of your life.

3.   Take a seat in a way that is comfortable for you. Rest your hands on your lap while you sit on a cushion or chair with your back straight.

4.   Close your eyes and take a few deep breaths. Pay attention to how you feel your breath coming in and going out. Let go of any tension with each exhale. Remember, there is no wrong way to do this, so just breathe.

5.   Pose the question or questions you would like to reflect on. For instance, "How can I improve myself?" or "What do I need to know about myself?"

6.   Let ideas come to mind without passing judgment. If you find that your thoughts are wandering, just gently redirect them to your breath.

7.   As you come to the end of your meditation, pause for a moment to consider what you have learned and how you feel about it.

8.   The insights and clarity received during meditation are gifts, and you should express your gratitude for them.

9.   Open your eyes when you feel ready.

Keeping a journal will help you develop this skill and teach you to grow!

Embrace Understanding Through Self-Reflection and Recognize Your Inner Power

Gaining insight into your inner workings is the first step in discovering and using your power. By intentionally and purposefully practicing self-reflection, or introspection, you gain a deeper understanding of the complex landscape of your inner world—your thoughts, feelings, and goals.

In the quiet moments of reflection, you give yourself permission to hear the soft murmurs of your soul. These whispers carry insights, desires, fears, and the essence of your true nature. Introspection serves as a mirror, reflecting the multifaceted parts of your personality.

A deeper understanding of your decisions and what drives you can be achieved through developing self-awareness, which in turn requires you to recognize patterns of behavior, triggers, and responses. It's not easy to embrace yourself, flaws and all, without passing judgment. Still, you can start to uncover your hidden power through self-reflection techniques like journaling, meditation, or professional therapy, and can begin unraveling the parts that stand in your way.

As you go through this slow and steady process, you will come to realize all the limitless potential within you. A deeper connection to your inner magic begins with this intentional approach. The more you discover about yourself—your unique combination of experiences, thoughts, and memories—the more doors open to the limitless potential within. The end goal is to learn and embrace all of your unique qualities, turning your weaknesses into strengths and transforming constraints into opportunities for personal development.

Bring an attitude of genuine curiosity and openness to this adventure, and your inner power will emerge.

The Foundation for Elemental Harmony

Connecting with the elemental energies that form the core of witchcraft is a natural progression from exploring your inner self. As we enter the domain of elemental magic and the balanced interaction of the elements, approach with the same curiosity and willingness to learn that you brought to discovering and exploring yourself.

The natural world is an integral part of witchcraft, and the elements— earth, air, fire, water, and spirit—are the sources of its power. Comprehending the mysterious symphony of the elements requires an understanding of their individual essences. Below, we will explore the qualities, correspondences, and magical properties of each one, guiding you to attune your energies with their rhythmic cadence.

The path to mastery begins with tuning in to the individual qualities of each element, like trying to make sense of this mystical symphony's very complex and varied notes.

Earth: Stability and Nourishment

The earth, which gives the magician both grounding and sustenance, is the center of attention in this symphony.

Explore the grounding properties of the earth and its rituals, which connect your energies to a solid foundation of stability. Lying down in the grass or on the earth is a wonderful way to ground after a spell or ritual, and can help dissipate any residual energies. The stones whisper old stories of toughness and resilience, and the rich soil turns into a blank canvas where you can paint your plans.

Air: Intellect and Ethereal Currents

Flowing smoothly through the symphony is air, which is linked to ethereal currents and mental processes. There are exercises that can help you tune in to the soft whispers of the winds. Some examples are meditation, breathing exercises, and powerful spells. Take a deep breath of the knowledge that the wind carries, and let out a sigh of relief for the clarity that fills the air.

Fire: Transformation and Passion

It is within the elemental symphony that the blazing notes of transformation and passion are ignited. Through rituals and candle magic that spark creativity and passion, we bring into focus the transformative dance of fire. In addition to bearing witness to the change, the flames, which embody the fire element, also serve as its catalyst.

Water: Emotions and Intuition

As the melodic rhythm reverberates, the calming sounds of water carry listeners away to a state of emotional release. Practices involving water, scrying, and intuition can help you navigate the depths of your emotions.

Spirit: At the Core

If earth is the root and foundation, then spirit is the ley lines, the conductor of it all—the threads that combine and bind all of the elements together.

Spirit, the essence that goes beyond the material, is central and encompasses all of the elements. It is through the spirit that we delve into the ethereal domain, practicing rituals and meditations to bring your soul into harmony with the cosmos.

True mastery and understanding of the elements requires the ability to read the lines they weave, which contain the attributes, correspondences, and magical powers of each element. Your magical repertoire expands as you learn to write, cast, and adapt spells that resonate with the rhythmic cadence of each element—and that resonate with you.

When it comes to witchcraft, you serve as both the *creator and created*, signing a mutually beneficial contract with the elements involved in channeling and creating magic. When you are working on spells, it is important to keep in mind that each element brings its own distinct energies to add to your intentions. Earth anchors, air amplifies, fire transforms, water flows, and spirit transcends. When all of these elemental forces come together, they synergize to form a powerful current that propels your desires into manifestation.

The Alchemy of Intentions

Before delving into the craft, understand that spellcasting is a form of alchemy—an art that transmutes the raw materials of intent into magical manifestations. There is an inherent value in your intentions, just like there is in precious metals. Your intentions are shaped and amplified by the elemental forces that lend their power to the process.

Begin your journey into witchcraft with simplicity. Your practice will be built on the foundation of simple rituals. Explore the correspondences between the elements, infuse your rituals with intention, and observe the subtle but profound shifts that ripple through the fabric of reality. It is not uncommon for the most straightforward spells to be among the most potent. That is precisely why I've included spells like these for you later in the book.

Reflect on the delicate balance required to harness the elements. Balance your inner energy with external forces to ensure a harmonious and potent practice.

Earth, the grounding force, anchors your practice instability. Being too grounded, though, might cause you to become stuck. Think about the harmony between stability and adaptability. You should be as steady as the old trees that sway in the wind, yet able to bend and change with the times.

The element air, which is associated with intelligence, may be heard whispering its secrets along the halls of your mind. However, a gust too strong may scatter your focus. Strike a balance between lucid thought and the ethereal flow. Allow the soft winds of inspiration to carry you forward while you hold fast to the firm ground below.

The transforming power of fire can be both a source of light and a devourer. Think on how to maintain a steady equilibrium between unbridled enthusiasm and controlled intensity in your magical workings.

Water, the conduit of emotions, beckons you to navigate its fluid currents. However, chaos can ensue if emotions run rampant. Strive for a balance between emotional steadiness and intuitive fluidity. Embrace the natural flow of your emotions as they carve out pathways to understanding and connection.

In the delicate balance lies the true magic—the alchemy that transforms intent into reality.

Prepare to unravel mysteries, discover your strengths, and learn how to connect with the witchcraft type that speaks to your soul. The "Witchcraft Type Quiz," which will reveal the distinct aspects of your magical identity, is waiting for you in Chapter 3.

Chapter 3:

Which Witch Are You? Identifying Your Witchcraft Path

As you embark on your journey of discovery, you might return to this chapter several times. The questions that follow are there to guide you, nudging you and illuminating your road toward identifying aspects that resonate most strongly with your inner witch.

This quiz will cover elements from Wicca, Traditional, Green, Kitchen, Hedge, Chaos, and Eclectic Witchcraft. As you work through these questions, take a moment to reflect on each one, as they delve into the nuanced aspects of magic as a whole. Your thoughtful responses will help unveil your unique connection to the world of witchcraft.

Each answer corresponds with a score: A = 1 point, B = 2 points, C = 3 points, D = 4 points, E = 5 points, and F = 0 points.

> For example:
>
> *Which element do you feel the strongest connection to?*
>
> > A. *Earth (1 point)*

B. *Air (2 points)*

C. *Fire (3 points)*

D. *Water (4 points)*

E. *All of the above (5 points)*

F. *None of the above (0 points)*

So, if you selected *C. Fire*, you'd award yourself 3 points for this question. Keep track of your score to reveal your witchcraft type at the end!

This Is Your Witchcraft Type Quiz

Question 1

Which element do you feel the strongest connection to?

A. Earth

B. Air

C. Fire

D. Water

E. All of the above

F. None of the above

Question 2

During which season do you feel most in tune with yourself and your magical practice?

A. Spring

B. Summer

C. Autumn

D. Winter

E. All of the above

F. None of the above

Question 3

When you spend time outdoors, which aspect of nature resonates with you the most?

A. The earth beneath my feet

B. The rustle of leaves in the wind

C. The warmth of the sunlight

D. The sound of flowing water

E. All of the above

F. None of the above

Question 4

Which magical tool appeals to you the most?

A. Athame (ritual knife)

B. Wand

C. Cauldron

D. Chalice

E. All of the above

F. None of the above

Question 5

Which type of spells do you find most appealing?

A. Practical spells for daily life

B. Intellectual and knowledge-seeking spells

C. Spells for emotional well-being

D. Transformation and empowerment spells

E. All of the above

F. None of the above

Question 6

Which divination tool speaks to you the most?

A. Tarot cards

B. Runes

C. Scrying

D. Pendulum

E. All of the above

F. None of the above

Question 7

How do you, or how do you want to, incorporate celestial bodies into your magical practice?

    A. Aligning with planetary influences

    B. Harnessing the power of stars and constellations

    C. Utilizing lunar energies

    D. Embracing solar energies

    E. All of the above

    F. None of the above

Question 8

Do you, or do you want to, work with specific animals or animal spirits in your practice?

    A. Yes, for guidance and grounding

    B. Yes, for intellectual insights and wisdom

    C. Yes, for emotional connections and intuition

    D. Yes, for transformative energies and symbolism

    E. All of the above

    F. None of the above

Question 9

Which type of spell ingredients do you find most appealing?

    A. Earthly herbs and roots

    B. Intellectual and symbolic components

    C. Emotional and intuitive elements

    D. Transformative and energetic materials

    E. All of the above

F. None of the above

Question 10

How often do you, or do you intend to, practice divination in your magical routine?

    A. Daily

    B. Weekly

    C. Monthly

    D. Seasonally

    E. All of the above

    F. None of the above

Question 11

How do you view the purpose of magic in your life?

    A. As a means of maintaining tradition and stability

    B. In the pursuit of knowledge and intellectual growth

    C. As a source of emotional healing and intuition

    D. As a catalyst for personal transformation and empowerment

    E. All of the above

    F. None of the above

Question 12

Which is your primary goal in practicing witchcraft?

A. Seeking stability and grounding

B. Acquiring knowledge and wisdom

C. Enhancing emotional well-being

D. Facilitating personal transformation

E. All of the above

F. None of the above

Question 13

Do you, or do you intend to, incorporate specific plants or herbs in your magical practice?

A. Yes, for grounding and stability

B. Yes, for intellectual and wisdom-seeking purposes

C. Yes, for emotional well-being and intuition

D. Yes, for transformative and energetic work

E. All of the above

F. None of the above

Question 14

Which moon phase do you find most appealing?

A. New moon

B. Waxing moon

C. Full moon

D. Waning moon

E. All of the above

F. None of the above

Question 15

How do you, or how do you intend to, create a sacred space for yourself and your magical workings?

A. Through traditional rituals and ceremonies

B. Through intellectual and symbolic arrangements

C. Through emotional and intuitive connection

D. Through transformative and personalized adaptations

E. All of the above

F. None of the above

Results

As you look below to get your result, you'll notice that some of the types overlap, since many witchcraft types share some commonalities. Just pick the one that most appeals to you first, or read both chapters in Part II and then decide. If neither feels right, consider Eclectic Witchcraft, which allows you to pick and choose a wide variety of witchcraft types depending on the spell, your mood, and your personality:

- **17–27 points:** Your witchcraft type leans toward Hedge Witchcraft.

- **24–46 points:** Your witchcraft type leans toward Kitchen Witchcraft.

- **36–48 point points:** Your witchcraft type leans toward

Wicca.

- **43 points:** Your witchcraft type leans toward Chaos Witchcraft.

- **46–51 points:** Your witchcraft type leans toward Green Witchcraft.

- **64–69 points:** Your witchcraft type leans toward Traditional Witchcraft.

- **0–75 points:** Your witchcraft type leans toward Eclectic Witchcraft. (Because of the nature of Eclectic Witchcraft, the score ranges from 0 to 75. So, if you find yourself leaning toward Eclectic Witchcraft over your actual result, you are invited to head to Chapter 10 to see if it aligns better with your soul.)

Part II of the book will go over each of the seven types of witchcraft in more detail.

Again, the result of this quiz is a starting point, a gentle nudge toward self-discovery. It is not a binding contract but an invitation to engage in other types of witchcraft. Feel free to browse through the chapters, following your curiosity and intuition. Or, simply retake the quiz.

Note: If any magical terms puzzle you, turn to the Glossary for clarification!

Part II:

Diving Deep into the

Witchcraft Paths

Chapter 4:
Wicca Unveiled–Rituals, Gods and Goddesses, Symbols

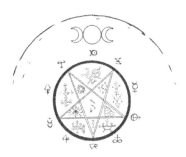

Whether you were brought here through the quiz or your natural curiosity, let's dive into the world of Wicca. If a deep connection for this witchcraft type resonates by the end, you've found your magical path. Otherwise, feel free to explore other types and chapters to discover what aligns with your spirit.

An Overview

At its core, Wicca revolves around the worship of nature, the celebration of cycles, and a deep connection to the divine. One of its distinguishing characteristics is the variety of practices it offers, which enables witches to personalize their spiritual journey while still adhering to a set of shared principles within their coven or community.

The origins of Wicca can be attributed to figures like Gerald Gardner and Doreen Valiente, who played pivotal roles in its development; the practice was also influenced by pre-Christian rituals, folklore, and ceremonial magic. Gardner is frequently referred to as the "father" of Wicca. He was the one who formalized the religion's rituals and practices, thereby laying the foundation for the flourishing and diverse Wiccan community that exists today.

Wiccans follow the Wheel of the Year, a year-long ritual that commemorates the passage of time and the sacredness of nature. This yearly cycle has eight Sabbats, or festivals, that indicate significant times in the year.

A combination of symbolism, magic, and spiritual expression is found in Wiccan rituals. A fundamental aspect of Wiccan practice is the casting of circles, which involves the creation of a sacred space for the purpose of communicating with the divine. Some of the elements that contribute to the transformative nature of these rituals include chanting, dance, and visualization. Through the practice of Esbats, which are lunar rituals, and Sabbats, which are seasonal celebrations, Wiccans align their magic with the natural cycles that occur throughout the year.

The divine is often represented as a dual deity—the God and the Goddess. The duality that is inherent in nature is embodied by this divine couple, who reflect aspects of creation, destruction, and rebirth into their makeup. By acknowledging a pantheon of gods and goddesses from a variety of traditions, Wiccans may choose particular deities to work with based on personal resonance, or they may choose to take a more eclectic approach.

Cernunnos and Brigid of the Celts, Odin and Freyja of the Norse, and Osiris and Isis of Egypt are some of the most common pairings.

Should you choose to work with deities or other entities, participating in rituals, invocations, or devotions can help you establish a connection with them. Developing a rapport with gods and goddesses requires familiarity with their myths, correspondences, and symbols, as well as the alignment of your goals with their characteristics. You can use this spiritual bond to strengthen your magical rituals and find your way in Wicca.

In the end, the god or goddess chosen is subjective and can be adjusted to suit your cultural background and spiritual views. Wicca teaches that you can gain a better knowledge of yourself and the environment by making contact with these deities.

Rituals, deities, and religious symbols are all laid bare in Wicca, which invites individuals to delve into a spiritual path that is at once ancient and modern. Its tenets, which have their origins in magic and nature, provide a platform for individual development and self-expression. A Wiccan's path leads them into a sacred realm where the divine dances with the changing seasons and where symbolism permeates every ritual.

A quick reminder to my dear readers: If at any point you feel adrift among terms that perplex you, I have created a Glossary at the end of the book that you can refer to!

Setting Up Your Space

A crucial part of spellwork and rituals is making sure your space is set up in a sacred and harmonious way. In order to connect with the divine and tap into the energies of nature, a Wiccan prepares their space before engaging in any magical practice.

The first step is to set up an altar, which is a place of spiritual energy and elemental symbolism.

It can be built on any surface, as long as it is sturdy and won't be disturbed by pets. It is the focus of your practice. Whatever your magical focus, you can cover your altar in a cloth. It can be any size and any color, and made of any fabric of your choice. Common items you can include are candles, athames or wands, representations of your chosen God and Goddess, and other ritual tools associated with your practice. Include symbolic items that speak to you in order to add your own personal touch.

Step-by-Step Guide to Casting a Circle

Step 1: Prepare your space

The circle you cast does not need to fill the whole space. For most, a circle just big enough for you and your altar is perfect. Choose a quiet space where you will be undisturbed during the ritual. Cleanse the area of any physical or energetic clutter.

Step 2: Gather your tools

Every spell will require different ingredients, tools, or other items. Once you know what spell you want to cast, you will know what tools you will need. Collect any tools or items you'll use for your ritual, such as candles and crystals, and don't forget your athame (or a wand if you don't have one).

Step 3: Set your intentions

Clarify your intentions for casting the circle. Are you creating a space for protection, focus, or ritual work? You can create a spell-targeted circle, or you can create a protection circle that you can keep open around your work area until you are done for the day.

Step 4: Ground yourself

Stand in the center of the space. Take a few deep breaths to center yourself. Visualize your energy reaching down into the earth and drawing strength and stability from nature.

Step 5: Call the quarters

Face each of the four cardinal directions (North, East, South, West) and invoke the corresponding element through your chosen item:

- North: earth (a small bowl of soil or a crystal)
- East: air (a feather or incense)
- South: fire (a candle)
- West: water (a bowl of water)

You can say a simple invocation, hum, or do this in reverent silence as you place each of these items in the designated spaces that correspond with their cardinal directions.

Step 6: Draw the circle

Use your athame to draw an energetic circle around you beginning at cardinal North. Visualize a sphere of energy forming as you do this.

Step 7: Create the boundaries

Envision the energy of the circle forming a protective barrier. This barrier keeps unwanted energies out and your magical energy in.

Step 8: Invoke your deities

If you work with deities, spirits, or specific entities, invite them to join you within the circle.

Step 9: State the purpose of the circle

Clearly state the purpose of the circle, whether it's for protection, focus, or specific ritual work. Intention binds the energies and focus together.

Step 10: Perform your magic

When you are ready, you can now cast your spells and rituals within your circle.

Step 11: Close the circle

When you have completed your magical workings, thank the energies you've invoked and dismiss them in reverse order (West, South, East, North). Release the energy of the circle by "cutting through" it with your athame. A simple cross flick will do the job.

Step 12: Final grounding and release

Take a few deep breaths and visualize any excess energy flowing back into the earth. This prevents lingering energies or cross-contamination with other spells.

Spells

All of your spells will require you to cast a circle before you begin. Ensure you have all of your needed materials and tools to do so, above and beyond what the spell itself calls for.

Note: Check out the "Witchy Products" page at the back of this book for a magical shopping experience, providing all the essential items and ingredients for your spells and rituals.

Protection Spell

What you will need:

- A white candle
- Salt
- A few sprigs of fresh rosemary

Incantation

Guardians of the watchtowers, I call on thee,

By Earth, Air, Fire, and Sea, protect and shield me.

Instructions

1. Cast your circle.

2. Place your white candle in the center of your space or altar. Ensure it is secured in a candle holder or placed firmly in a fireproof dish so it will not cause a fire.

3. Create a salt circle around your candle, invoking the spirits of protection.

4. Light the candle while envisioning energies of protection enveloping you or the target of your spell.

5. Repeat your incantation as you place the sprigs of rosemary around your candle.

6. Allow the candle to burn out.

7. Close your circle when your spell is complete.

Prosperity Talisman

What you will need:

- A green candle
- Cinnamon oil
- Small pouch
- Coins

Incantation

Abundance flows, my spirit's decree,

So shall it be, as I will, blessed be.

Instructions

1. Cast your circle.

2. Anoint your green candle with cinnamon oil while focusing on your goal of prosperity.

3. Place your candle in the center of your space or altar. Ensure it is secured in a candle holder or placed firmly in a fireproof dish for safety.

4. Light the candle and visualize abundance flowing into your life.

5. As the candle burns, repeat your incantation. Take your coins and pass them through the flame of the candle.

6. Place your coins in the small pouch and carry it with you through your day.

7. Safely extinguish the candle.

8. Close your circle when your spell is complete.

Self-Love Spell

What you will need:

- A pink candle
- A small rhodonite crystal
- Rose oil
- Carving tool

Incantation

By Earth, Air, Fire, and Sea,

I conjure self-love within me.

As the moon above does shine,

Let self-compassion now be mine.

Instructions

1. Cast your circle.

2. Carve the words "I embrace myself fully" or a similar phrase into the side of your candle. It does not need to be pretty, so don't stress about it being perfect.

3. Anoint your candle with the rose oil.

4. Place your candle in the center of your space or altar. Make sure your candle is secured in a candle holder or placed firmly in a fireproof dish for safety.

5. Light the candle and repeat your incantation. Envision a

warm, pink light surrounding you, radiating self-love.

6. Place the rhodonite crystal in front of the candle and focus on it.

7. Allow the energies of self-love to flow through you. Repeat your incantation if you feel the need.

8. Safely extinguish the candle.

9. Close your circle when your spell is complete.

10. Carry the rhodonite crystal with you to bring that same self-love energies into your daily life.

*****

Once you have worked your way through the spells here, I suggest looking into some of the other types of witchcraft. Even if you don't read this book in sequential order, do finish with the Conclusion.

You can also look forward to a book dedicated solely to Wicca in the near future! Sign up to be notified of its release (and others in the series) and receive a free Wicca spell! Just enter the link below into your browser or scan the QR code on the following page:

https://www.unleashingyourinnerwitch.com/get-notified

Chapter 5:
Traditional Witchery–Methods, Beliefs, Practices

Traditional Witchcraft is where many new witches first get exposed to the magical world. Whether it was through the quiz or you were simply and inexplicably drawn to this chapter, you've found your magical path.

While it is usually good to go with your first instinctual feeling, if this chapter does not *quite* resonate, you are always invited to explore the other types of witchcraft to discover what truly aligns with your spirit.

An Overview

Traditional Magic includes a wide range of magical practices that have their roots in history, culture, or family. This broad category includes folk magic, which is made up of rituals that have been passed down through generations in certain communities. These rituals are usually told orally and are based on local traditions.

Traditional Magic comes from the shared knowledge of a group of people, whether it is practiced in a family, a rural area, or a specific cultural group. It shows how those people feel about spirituality, values, and the supernatural forces that affect their lives. Keeping magical traditions alive and changing them over time is what Traditional Magic is all about—much like folk magic.

Traditional Magic is inherently tied to folk magic, as it represents the enduring magical practices and beliefs that have been sustained within a cultural or familial context. Traditional Magic, in essence, is a broader term that includes folk magic as a subset. It includes the traditions and knowledge that have been passed down from generation to generation and are deeply rooted in the culture of a community.

In the practice of Traditional Witchcraft, it is common for witches to place a strong emphasis on their ancestry, drawing upon the knowledge and rituals that have been passed down from one generation to the next. There is a possibility that this connection will involve paying homage to ancestors, working with family traditions, or incorporating folk magic from various parts of the witch's region.

Folk magic, which frequently involves the use of spells, charms, and rituals designed to provide protection, is one of the defining characteristics of Traditional Witchcraft. In addition, herbology plays a significant role because practitioners in this field make use of the magical properties of herbs for the purposes of medicine, divination, and the casting of spells.

While there is some overlap between this facet of traditional witchcraft and the practices of the Green Witch (covered in Chapter 6), they differ in their emphasis and focus. The Green Witch primarily centers on herbalism, nature-based spirituality, and a deep connection with the natural world. By contrast, Traditional Witchcraft, while often incorporating elements of nature, places a broader emphasis on various magical practices, rituals, and cultural influences passed down through generations. The two share a common thread of working with magical energies but diverge in their specific areas of concentration and the depth of their ties to tradition.

Traditional Witches frequently have a profound respect for the natural world, which is often regarded as a source of divine power and knowledge. The cycles of the moon, the changes that take place throughout the seasons, and other elements of the natural world are all considered to be essential components in accordance with their traditional spiritual beliefs.

Scrying, tarot reading, and rune casting are all examples of divination techniques (see the Glossary) that are frequently utilized by Traditional Witches in the practice of their craft. These practices are instruments that can be utilized to acquire understanding, guidance, and insights into things that are not visible to the naked eye.

Within the umbrella of Traditional Witchcraft, there is the potential for a diverse array of belief systems to exist. Some practitioners may adhere to a polytheistic approach, which is characterized by the honoring of multiple deities. On the other hand, others may have a tendency to adhere to pantheism, which is characterized by the belief that the divine is pre-existing in all aspects of nature.

It is essential for witches to take into account the importance of ethics and responsibility when it comes to the practice of magic. Many people adhere to a code of magical ethics that reveres natural equilibrium and places an emphasis on the utilization of magic for constructive purposes. This code is followed by a significant number of people.

Creating and carrying out rituals is an essential part of Traditional Witchcraft. These rituals are frequently modified to cater to the specific needs of the individual or to commemorate a specific occasion. Some of the rituals that fall under this category include the casting of spells, the practice of meditation, and communication with the spirits.

Traditional Witches frequently draw their inspiration from sacred sites and the folklore of their communities. Natural landmarks, ancient ruins, and locations said to be associated with local legends are all examples of possible locations for these sites. Folklore is a rich source of traditions and symbolism that are considered to be associated with magic.

There is a deep respect for the mysteries of the craft, a reverence for the traditions that have been passed down through the generations, and a celebration of the magical potential that can be found in everyday life.

Setting Up Your Space

Traditional Witches create their sacred space for witchcraft with great care and devotion. The altar is the focal point, bearing symbols of the elements, sacred tools, and items of personal significance. Candles and herbs are carefully chosen to invoke specific magical outcomes. The casting of a circle, a fundamental practice, marks the sacred boundary of the witch's space. With respect for tradition, each tool is placed with purpose, creating a space where energies converge in harmony.

Here are some basic rituals, their purposes, and the tools you will need to complete them.

Cleanse Your Space

Purpose

Purify and prepare your space for magical workings.

Tools

A smudge bundle or stick (cedar, palo santo, or rosemary) and a white feather (you can also use your hand).

Ritual

Light the smudge bundle or stick and use the feather to waft the smoke throughout your space, going in a clockwise pattern. As you do, visualize any negative or stagnant energy dissipating as the smoke rises. Focus on your intention of cleansing and inviting magic into your space. There is no need to rush. When you are done, extinguish your bundle.

Charge Your Crystals

Purpose

Cleanse and enhance the energy of your crystals.

Tools

Crystals of your choice.

Ritual

Place your crystals on a windowsill or outside during a sunny day or under the light of the moon. Visualize the energy of the sun or moon infusing the crystals with their respective energies, enhancing their magical properties. Other crystals can be placed under running water or buried in the soil (just be sure your crystal won't be damaged by this—opals are one of those that cannot be placed in water).

Create Your Moon Water

Purpose

Harness the energy of the moon for magical workings.

Tools

A clean jar or bowl, spring or purified water, and a clear quartz crystal.

Ritual

Pour the water into the container of your choice and set it under the light of the moon (the stage of the moon determines the energy you want to harness—you can learn more in the Glossary!). Add the clear quartz crystal to infuse the water with lunar energy. Let it sit overnight, and in the morning, before sunrise, collect your water. Now your moon water is ready for use in spells or rituals.

Spells

Spellwork is defined by a unique blend of simplicity and complexity. Every component of a spell, from the tools to the ingredients, has a story to tell and is important in its own right. The simplicity lies in a ritualistic and methodical approach, drawing from traditions.

The ability to tune in to the energies involved, master the connections, and respect ancestral wisdom is woven into every part of the craft. It is a balance between the straightforward and the nuanced layers that gives Traditional Magic its lasting power.

An important reminder, however, is that with any spell, especially those for personal gain, it is very important to be mindful of the concept of natural equilibrium. A positive outcome for you may cause an equal and opposite outcome somewhere else in the field, so be sure to exercise caution.

Note: Check out the "Witchy Products" page at the back of this book for a magical shopping experience, providing all the essential items and ingredients for your spells and rituals.

Warding Ritual for Home Protection

What you will need:

- 4 black candles
- 4 small black tourmaline or quartz crystals
- Salt
- 1 tsp dried rosemary
- 1 tsp ground cinnamon
- 1 tsp dried basil
- 1 tsp ground bay leaves
- Athame or wand

Instructions

1. Set your intention.

2. Combine the salt and herbs.

3. Place your black candles (in holders or fireproof dishes) in cardinal points (i.e., North, East, South, and West) in your home, also placing a crystal in front of each candle.

4. Sprinkle the herb and salt mixture at the entrances or boundaries of your home. These can be actual entrances or demarcated private areas. You can also use the perimeter of your home as a boundary.

5. Using your athame or wand, draw your protective sigils (see Chapter 9 and the Glossary) in the air at these boundaries, creating a shield of protection against negative forces.

6. Return to your candles and light them, ensuring you focus on your intention of protecting and securing your home.

7. As you bring the ritual to a close, express gratitude to the gods or spirits you called upon for protection and picture the protective barrier forming around your home.

Full Moon Prosperity Jar

What you will need:

- Jar
- Charged crystal
- A pinch of fresh basil leaves
- 1 tsp ground cinnamon
- Coin
- Moon water charged under a full moon

Instructions

1. The first step is to purify and bless your jar. You can do this by holding it over the smoke from a candle or incense stick, or giving it a quick rinse in running water. Add your various items to the jar. Add the crystal last.

2. Fill the jar with moon water. Focus on your intention to bring about abundance and prosperity.

3. Place the container in a spot that you associate with prosperity or money, like your office or an area where you handle finances.

Moon Phase Wish Fulfillment Spell

Pick a moon phase that corresponds to your goal (a new moon is associated with new beginnings, a full moon with completion and manifestation—see the Glossary for a short description of the moon phases).

What you will need:

- Pen and paper
- A candle (choose a color that corresponds with your wish—see the Glossary)
- A fire-safe bowl

Instructions

1. Set up your candle in the center of your altar or working space, and place the fire-safe bowl nearby.

2. Be specific about what you desire. Use precise and optimistic language; avoid leaving room for misunderstanding. Write it

down on your piece of paper.

3. As you light the candle, focus on the flame. Imagine the energy of the fire sparking the manifestation of your wish.

4. Carefully hold the paper with your wish over the flame of the candle, allowing it to catch fire. Place the burning paper in the fire-safe bowl.

5. Just picture your wish dissolving into smoke as the paper burns, and your intentions floating up into the sky.

6. Speak out loud or mentally restate and reaffirm your desire as you observe the paper burn.

7. Once the paper has turned to ash, dispose of it in a way that feels right to you. Some people choose to bury it, while others prefer to scatter it in the wind.

8. Express gratitude to your gods, the elements, or the universe for listening to your wishes and making them come true.

*****

Once you've immersed yourself in the spells, I invite you to explore other witchcraft types that beckon to you (be sure to read the Conclusion, even if you're not following the book in order!).

Quick note: You can look forward to a book that will focus solely on Traditional Witchcraft and other related titles in the near future! To get a free spell and join the early notification list, just enter the link into your browser or scan the QR code on the next page.

https://www.unleashingyourinnerwitch.com/get-notified

Chapter 6:

The Green Witch–Connecting With Nature Spirits

Whether it's the energies of the Green Witch that have drawn you in or you arrived here via the quiz, welcome. You are in for an extraordinary, fulfilling adventure. However, if you read through this chapter and find that Green Magic doesn't ring true to your soul, I invite you to explore the other types of witchcraft in this book until you find the one that speaks to your heart.

An Overview

The Green Witch embodies a deep and profound connection with the natural world. Herbalism, earth-centered spirituality, and a dedication to living an environmentally responsible life are the foundations upon which the Green Witch builds a path that is in harmony with both the cycles of the natural world and the spirits that inhabit it.

Green Witches are herbalists at heart, using the magical properties of plants for healing, spellcraft, and rituals. They cultivate their own magical gardens, tending to herbs with intention and reverence.

These witches actively seek to connect with nature spirits—be they spirits of trees, water, or the land itself. This involves practices such as meditation, offerings, and rituals to honor and communicate with the unseen inhabitants of the natural world.

Leaving a token of gratitude for a tree or performing a water ceremony by a stream are examples of regular practices that involve offerings. By performing these rituals, Green Witches strengthen the connection they have with the spirits they wish to honor.

The elements of earth, air, fire, and water also play a significant role in Green Witchcraft. Green Witches regularly work with the energies of these elements, invoking their presence in rituals, and attuning oneself to the subtle influences they have.

Due to the reverence Green Witches have for the natural world, they acknowledge the presence of the divine in every flower, stone, and breeze. The interconnectedness of all living things is something that they believe in, and they make it a goal to live in harmony with the earth. The majority of people who practice animism acknowledge the spiritual essence present in all facets of nature. The Green Witch believes that the land is a living, breathing entity that possesses its own spirit, and a significant part of their practice involves actively engaging with these spirits.

To do this, they immerse themselves in the natural world, paying close attention to the nuances that are present in their surroundings. The practice of nature walks, which can take place within dense forests or in the midst of beautiful gardens, can be used to achieve the goals of meditation and communion with the spirits of the land.

Fittingly, elements of nature are used in the divination rituals of the Green Witch. The interpretation of the flight of birds, the reading of patterns in the wind, and the use of natural objects such as stones and leaves are all examples of potential methods of divination.

Green Witches, with their deep-rooted connection to nature spirits, celebrate the sacredness of the earth. Not only does the Green Witch perform a craft, they also become a steward of the natural world by practicing herbalism and elemental magic and making a commitment to living in harmony with the land. At the heart of Green Witchcraft lies the recognition that every breeze carries a message, every rustle of leaves speaks of magic, and every footstep in nature is a dance with the spirits of the earth.

Herbs and Plants

There is a central focus on the sacred dance with nature in the world of Green Witchcraft. Sorcery is an ode to nature, concocted by a witch who knows the rhythms of the planet and who makes use of plants for their healing abilities. Every herb and plant has its own unique magical purpose and set of characteristics.

As part of their rituals, Green Witches develop a close bond with various plants and harness their energies to create a harmonious and healing sacred space that manifests their thoughts and desires. Mastery of the three levels of herb and plant properties—primary, secondary, and tertiary—is crucial in the complex practice of magical herbalism.

Primary, Secondary, and Tertiary Properties

When it comes to witchcraft and magic, although there isn't a universally accepted definition of what constitutes "primary," "secondary," or "tertiary" magical features, there is still a general common understanding in the community. The following is my understanding of the terms, which should serve you well as a solid foundation for further exploration.

Primary Magical Properties

The primary magical properties of a plant are those most commonly associated with it.

For example, one of the primary magical properties of lavender is its ability to induce feelings of relaxation and calmness. The fact that this magical property is widely used and is considered common knowledge is what makes it a primary magical property.

Secondary Magical Properties

An herb or plant can also have secondary magical properties, which are additional qualities or associations that it may possess. These properties typically extend beyond the herb or plant's primary and most common uses.

Let's take lavender as an example again. A secondary magical property of lavender could be its association with the enhancement of psychic abilities. This would be a continuation of the primary property of lavender, which is relaxation. Even though relaxation is more widely recognized, some practitioners may believe that this secondary quality of lavender (in this case, the enhancement of psychic abilities) is just as significant as relaxation. However, since this property is not as commonly used, it becomes categorized as a secondary magical property.

Tertiary Magical Properties

Tertiary magical properties are even more specific and have a lower level of recognition in the magical community, in contrast to primary and secondary magical properties.

Again, let's use lavender. A tertiary magical property of lavender may be linked to the improvement of harmony and communication among individuals. Since this magical property is not as commonly or widely recognized within the community as either a primary or secondary magical property, it would fall into the tertiary category.

It is crucial to bear in mind that magical properties can differ from one culture or tradition to another. Some practitioners may place a property in the primary category, while others may place it in the secondary or tertiary categories. The magical powers of plants and herbs are often best understood through a mix of anecdotal evidence, historical context, personal experience, and intuitive knowledge.

Green Witches need to familiarize themselves with the properties of herbs and plants beyond traditional beliefs. It is also important to be aware of their powers according to your own beliefs and experiences before using them in magical practices.

10 Simple Herbs for Your Spells

Basil (*Ocimum basilicum*)

Basil is a versatile herb with a pleasant aroma. It's easy to grow in pots or garden beds and is known for its culinary uses and protective properties.

Basil is associated with protection, love, and prosperity. It's often used in rituals to attract positive energy and ward off negative influences.

Mint (*Mentha* spp.)

Mint is a hardy herb that comes in various varieties, such as peppermint and spearmint. It thrives in both sunlight and shade, making it a great choice for beginners.

Mint is linked to healing, purification, and prosperity. It's used in spells to promote good health, attract abundance, and purify spaces.

Rosemary (*Rosmarinus officinalis*)

Rosemary is a fragrant herb with a woody scent. It prefers well-drained soil and can be grown in pots or directly in the garden.

Rosemary is associated with protection, memory enhancement, and purification. It's often used in rituals for clarity or remembrance, and to ward off negativity.

Lavender (*Lavandula* spp.)

Lavender is known for its calming fragrance and beautiful purple flowers. It's a resilient plant that thrives in sunny conditions and well-drained soil.

Lavender is connected to love, relaxation, and purification. It's commonly used in spells for calming energy, promoting love, and enhancing psychic abilities.

Chamomile (*Matricaria chamomilla*)

Chamomile is a gentle herb with small, daisy-like flowers. It's easy to grow and is often used for its calming properties in teas and spells related to relaxation.

Chamomile is linked to relaxation, sleep, and purification. It's used in spells for tranquility, promoting restful sleep, and removing negative energy.

Thyme (*Thymus vulgaris*)

Thyme is a low-maintenance herb that adds flavor to culinary dishes. It's drought-tolerant and can be grown in containers or in the ground.

Thyme is associated with courage, strength, and purification. It's used in rituals for courage and energy, and to cleanse spaces of negativity.

Sage (*Salvia officinalis*)

Sage is a sacred herb with purifying properties. It's relatively easy to grow and can be used both in the kitchen and for ritualistic purposes.

Sage is known for its purifying and cleansing properties. It's used in rituals to clear negative energies, protect against harm, and promote wisdom.

Aloe vera (*Aloe barbadensis miller*)

Aloe is a succulent known for its soothing gel. It thrives in bright, indirect sunlight and well-drained soil.

Aloe vera is linked to healing, protection, and luck. It's used in spells for physical healing, soothing energy, and attracting good fortune.

Calendula (*Calendula officinalis*)

Calendula, also known as marigold, produces vibrant orange or yellow flowers. It's easy to grow and is often used in herbal skincare products and magical rituals.

Calendula is associated with joy, protection, and psychic abilities. It's used in rituals for enhancing intuitive powers, attracting positive energy, and promoting joy.

Dill (*Anethum graveolens*)

Dill is an annual herb with feathery leaves and small yellow flowers. It's a great addition to herb gardens and is commonly used in culinary applications.

Dill is linked to love, protection, and prosperity. It's used in spells to attract love, protect against negative influences, and enhance financial well-being.

Additional Care Instructions

Now that you've established a thriving green haven with your carefully tended plants, let's delve into the nourishing heart of your garden—composting and fertilizing.

For most herbs, like basil, mint, rosemary, thyme, sage, and dill, a balanced, all-purpose fertilizer works well. Apply your fertilizer in spring when new growth starts, and then once or twice more throughout the growing season.

- **Lavender:** Prefers slightly alkaline soil. Add lime to increase soil pH if needed.

- **Chamomile:** Doesn't require heavy feeding. A layer of compost in spring is usually sufficient.

- **Aloe vera:** Use a cactus or succulent fertilizer during the growing season. Fertilize sparingly.

- **Calendula:** A general-purpose fertilizer with balanced

nutrients is suitable.

These are a handful of popular and well-loved herbs for Green Witches. If you feel overwhelmed by all of this, start small. A potted lavender plant is easy to grow and maintain, and smells absolutely wonderful blowing in with the afternoon breeze.

Just between you and me, while growing things can be fun, it can also be a little time-consuming! So you will find no judgment from me if you choose to buy your herbs fresh or dried.

Setting Up Your Space

A Green Witch's path begins with the creation of a sacred place that is in harmony with the earth's natural energies. This can be a place you create specifically inside your own home, or somewhere outside. The magical sanctuary you create will serve as a nexus where intention meets the essence of green magic. Here you will create an altar with elemental symbols, honor plant allies, and participate in rituals that celebrate the natural world's cyclical rhythms.

Altar Setup

Set up your altar in a special place, ideally somewhere bright and airy. This would preferably be outside, but if you don't have access, or have very limited space, a room with plenty of windows or natural light is a good substitute.

Cover your altar with a green or earthy-colored cloth to symbolize nature. It can be any shape or size.

Arrange representations of the four elements: a small bowl of soil or stones (earth), a feather or incense (air), a candle (fire), and a bowl of water (water). You can also use small glass jars. For added power, crystals that are associated with earth energy, such as jade, green aventurine, or moss agate, are very valuable. You can be creative. Make this space resonate with you as well as with the energies of the earth.

Use seasonal décor to set the mood in your home. Leaves in the autumn, flowers in the spring, and seashells in the summer are some examples.

Change the decorations so they correspond with the Wheel of the Year and the changing of the seasons.

Herbs and Plants

You can decorate your space with potted plants, bringing the refreshing energy of nature indoors. These green companions not only add aesthetic appeal but also contribute to the overall vitality of your space.

You can also consider filling your space with the aroma of dried herbs. Arrange them in sachets, bundles, or bowls strategically placed throughout your home or around your altar. This not only enhances the ambiance but also provides a practical and visually appealing way to incorporate the magical properties of herbs into your spellwork and rituals.

Crystals and Candles

Make use of crystals to amplify your intentions or to draw upon the specific magical properties they possess. Each crystal carries its own vibration, aligning with different aspects of the natural world and various energies. For instance, amethyst may enhance spiritual growth and intuition, while rose quartz could channel energies of love and healing.

By strategically placing these crystals in your magical space or incorporating them into your rituals, you tap into their inherent magic.

Candles, on the other hand, provide a tangible link to the element of fire—a powerful force in spellcasting. Lighting candles during rituals invokes the transformative energy of fire and serves as a focal point for concentration and intention-setting.

Green candles, in particular, hold special significance in witchcraft. They are commonly used in spells that bring about growth, prosperity, and healing. As a symbol of life and growth, abundance, and nature, green is a powerful color. Using these candles in your magical rituals can help your spells work more effectively by bringing them into harmony with the energies you wish to attract.

Incense, Oils, and Offerings

Expressing your gratitude to the elements and spirits in your magical space is a sacred act that fosters a harmonious connection with the energies that surround you. Offering gifts is a tangible way to acknowledge and reciprocate the presence and assistance of these mystical forces.

Nature spirits particularly appreciate small offerings that reflect the natural world. Consider placing a bowl of fresh water, a handful of grains, or vibrant flowers as tokens of your appreciation.

Another thoughtful gesture is to provide live potted plants—an embodiment of the earth element. Remember to care for these plants as a continuous expression of your gratitude. These particular offerings will not be used in your spellwork, as they are intended as gifts!

Enhance your practice by incorporating various scents through oils and incense. Infusing the air with these fragrances adds an additional sensory dimension as well as serving as an offering to the spirits, creating a delightful and spiritually charged atmosphere. Choose scents that resonate with your intentions and the energies you wish to invoke, making your magical space a haven of gratitude and connection.

Spells and Rituals

The natural world is more than a backdrop for a Green Witch; it is an infinite wellspring of energy. These sacred rituals—whether you are sitting by a river, strolling through the woods, or just feeling the gentle touch of the wind on your skin—connect you deeply with nature and enhance your enchanted essence.

Any contact with nature has the capacity to bring about a miraculous metamorphosis!

Nature is a grand ritual in and of itself. Standing barefoot on the earth or bringing intention to your daily walk are both practices that can help you ground yourself and connect with the natural forces around you.

You can incorporate simple, everyday spells into your connection with nature without worrying about making them too complex. The Green Witch embraces the notion that every intention—indeed, every whispered desire—can be manifested through the connections you build with the elements.

Whispering a spell into the wind, making a potion with herbs you have foraged, or infusing your surroundings with intention while going for a stroll are all ways to cast a spell. It is clear to the Green Witch that spellwork is more than just certain rituals; it is about living in harmony with nature.

We Start With Protection

The initiation into spellcasting *always* begins with a fundamental and crucial starting point—a protection spell. This serves as an important keystone to your witchcraft practice and future spellwork.

It provides a shield of energy that safeguards you from unwanted influences and negativity. Protection spells are the gatekeepers of the mystical world, creating a barrier that allows only positive energies to enter your magical space.

When you begin with a protection spell, the significance lies not only in the fact that it provides a shield but also in the symbolism that it carries for you. It signifies your commitment to creating a space that is not only magically potent but also secure and attuned to your intentions.

By casting your first protection spell, you are doing more than just setting up a magical barrier; you are embracing the magical and claiming mastery over the energies that surround you.

Green Witch Protection Spell

What you will need:

- A small pouch
- Bay leaves
- Sage

- Rosemary
- Clear quartz crystal

Incantation

Quartz crystal, pure and bright,

Guard this space day and night.

Instructions

1. While visualizing the protective energy of each herb, place the bay leaves, sage, and rosemary in the pouch.

2. Hold the clear quartz crystal and charge it with your intention to create a protective aura by repeating the incantation above.

3. Place the crystal in the pouch with the herbs, and close the pouch tightly.

4. Carry the pouch with you for personal protection.

Green Witch Abundance Spell

What you will need:

- Basil leaves
- Mint leaves
- A cinnamon stick
- A green candle
- Fireproof dish or candle holder

Incantation

Basil's blessings, mint's sweet song,

In this dance, abundance belongs.

Cinnamon's desire, dreams ignite,

By earth and herb, my wish takes flight.

Instructions

1. Place the candle in the center of the fireproof dish, or ensure that it is firmly in the candle holder on a stable surface.

2. Sprinkle the mint and basil leaves around the candle, ensuring the candle is completely encircled.

3. Place the cinnamon stick in front of the candle, on top of the circle of herbs, ensuring it isn't broken.

4. As you light the candle, let your thoughts dwell on the abundant harvest you desire in specific areas of your life, then repeat the incantation.

5. Relax and let your thoughts wander to the realization of your abundant desires as the candle burns down.

Green Witch Healing Spell

What you will need:

- Lavender
- Chamomile
- Fresh eucalyptus leaves, or eucalyptus oil
- A blue or purple candle
- Fireproof dish or candle holder

Incantation

Lavender's peace, chamomile's embrace,

Eucalyptus gathers healing grace.

By earth's tender hold and herb's decree,

Healing energies, flow generously.

Instructions

1. Mix the lavender and chamomile together, infusing them with calming and healing energy.

2. You can either anoint the candle with eucalyptus oil or place fresh eucalyptus leaves around the base of the candle.

3. If you've used the oil, roll the anointed candle in the lavender and chamomile.

4. Carefully set it on a fireproof dish or ensure that it is firmly in the candle holder on a stable surface. If you are using fresh eucalyptus, place it around the fireproof dish instead.

5. As you light the candle, bring your attention to the calming and invigorating qualities of the herbs.

6. Picture yourself or the person you are casting the spell for being surrounded by healing energy as you recite the above incantation aloud.

*****

Note: Should any of the magical terms or items leave you a little confused, the Glossary is available for clarification! Check out the "Witchy Products" page at the back of this book for a magical shopping experience, providing all the essential items and ingredients for your spells and rituals. Also, a reminder that no matter how you navigate Part II of this book, make sure you finish your reading with the Conclusion.

You can look forward to a book dedicated solely to Green Witchcraft in the near future! Get a free spell just for signing up for our early notification list. Just enter the link below into your browser or scan the QR code.

https://www.unleashingyourinnerwitch.com/get-notified

Chapter 7:

The Kitchen Witch–Cooking Up Magic

Welcome home, Kitchen Witch. Whether you've been called here by the echoes of destiny, the light of your own curiosity, or the discovery of your witchcraft type, I invite you to bask in the warmth of the Kitchen Witch's hearth. Now, if for some reason the charm of culinary magic does not excite you, listen to your intuition and explore the other chapters, paying close attention to the witchcraft type that most resonates with your being.

An Overview

The Kitchen Witch is a practitioner who seamlessly blends the culinary arts with their magical practices. With a background in homemaking and a passion for the fire, Kitchen Witches bring their magical powers to every step of the cooking process, turning ordinary ingredients into extraordinary feasts.

Every dish becomes a magical creation. The choice of herbs, spices, and even cooking technique is dictated by the magical result they aim to achieve, as they infuse every ingredient with intent.

They are able to create a symphony of flavors and energies by the skillful combination of various herbs, spices, and food items, each of which possesses specific magical properties. The act of cooking is a sacred ritual. Every single step is imbued with a sense of enchantment, from the act of stirring in a clockwise direction to foster positive energy to the act of blessing ingredients with gratitude.

Kitchen Witches believe that food has the ability to provide nourishment not only to the body but also to the spirit. They consider cooking to be a spiritual act, a means of establishing a connection with the elements and infusing their creations with love and awareness of her intentions. The hearth and home are sacred spaces, and Kitchen Witches believe that a well-tended home and a lovingly prepared meal can be sources of comfort, healing, and protection.

Small altars, adorned with symbols, candles, and crystals, are created by some witches and placed in their kitchens. These altars serve as focal points for magic and a reminder of the sacredness of the culinary arts. Ingredients are not just chosen; they are carefully selected, blessed, and charged with energy. The Kitchen Witch's intentions are energetically imprinted in every ingredient, from a pinch of salt to a more complex ritual.

A well-cooked meal can do wonders for your spirit. A sense of belonging and camaraderie is fostered through the sharing of food because the Kitchen Witch knows it is a medium for the exchange of vitality, affection, and purpose.

Within the realm of Kitchen Witchcraft, the essence of magic can be found in the aroma of simmering herbs and the sound of a pan sizzling. Cooking becomes its own form of spellcraft, and every meal is an offering to the spirit and the senses. By transforming the mundane activity of cooking into a delightful blend of flavors, energies, and enchantment, the Kitchen Witch encourages you to embrace the magic that exists within your very own kitchen.

Mindful Practice

Kitchen Witchcraft calls on you to be mindful of your thoughts and intentions more than any of the other types of witchcraft.

As you chop herbs or stir the cauldron, practice mindfulness and bring yourself fully into the here and now. Each scent, sound, and touch beckons you to immerse yourself in the moment, imbuing your creations with magic and purpose.

This serves as the key to unlocking the full potential of your magical endeavors. As you embark on this journey, cultivating mindfulness allows you to be fully present in each magical act, infusing your intentions with purpose and power.

Here's a Quick How-To to Get You Started

This guided mindfulness practice serves as a foundation for developing a profound connection with the magical world around you, allowing you to navigate the intricacies of witchcraft with intention, awareness, and growth:

1. **Ground yourself:** Begin by grounding yourself in the present moment. Find a quiet place that is comfortable for

you. Take a few deep breaths, allowing the worries of the day to dissipate. Simply feel the earth beneath you as you breathe.

2. **Choose an energy focal point:** Select a magical tool or ingredient as your focal point. Choose something from your practice that captivates you—it could be a crystal, a herb, or anything else. Hold it in your hands, feeling its energy and weight.

3. **Observe with intent:** Observe the color, texture, and any other intricate details. As you do, let your mind still, allowing space for a deepened connection and an openness to experiencing an interplay of energy.

4. **Reflect on the magical significance:** Take into consideration the symbolism of the object you are holding in your hands. Think about its historical applications, the associations it has with the elements, and any symbolic meanings it may have.

5. **Set intentions:** When you understand an item better, you know how to best use it in your practice. Set an intention for its use in your craft. Whether it's for protection, clarity, or manifestation, visualize your intention infusing into the item, creating a harmonious resonance.

6. **Express gratitude:** Express gratitude for the energies present. Acknowledge the interconnectedness between yourself and the magical world.

7. **Incorporate mindfulness within your craft:** Bring the awareness you gained from this practice to every spell you cast as you progress through your witchcraft rituals. Whether you are in the kitchen, casting spells, or participating in a ritual, bring your whole attention to the

task at hand and know that the magic you have been working on is helping you manifest your intentions.

Setting Up Your Space

With an intuitive understanding of the magical properties of herbs, spices, and cooking techniques, Kitchen Witches approach their craft with both skill and intention. The desired magical outcome informs every decision, from the choice of herbs adorning the spice rack to the precise method of preparation. They recognize that the act of cooking is not merely a physical process but a sacred ritual, an opportunity to infuse each ingredient with purpose and energy.

Your magical journey begins long before the first flame is lit and the water is set to boil. It starts with the mindful selection of ingredients, chosen not only for their culinary appeal but also for the specific energies they bring.

The key is to create a space that feels both magical and practical for the act of cooking and crafting in the kitchen. Your space is also a reflection of your personal practice, so feel free to adapt and customize it based on your individual preferences and beliefs.

Imagine for a moment:

Bundles of sage, thyme, and rosemary hang delicately from twine, releasing a rich blend of earthy scents into the air as they dry. Beneath the hanging herbs, a mortar and pestle sits ready for its next culinary task. The carefully gathered dried chamomile flowers hold the potential to create healing draughts and concoctions that might soothe the body as well as the spirit.

A small altar nestled among the culinary chaos is a testament to the blending of the mundane and the mystical. Your recipe book, a unique Book of Shadows, lies open beside it, ready to impart its secrets.

This is the home and altar of the Kitchen Witch—and now yours too, if you feel drawn to it.

Your Tools

In the kitchen, magic thrives in the ordinary. Through the intentional use of everyday tools, you elevate your cooking routine into a sacred act, making each meal a manifestation of your magical prowess.

Everyday kitchen utensils like knives, spoons, and pots can be magically charged for cooking spells, transforming them into magical conduits and powerful tools. Put some thought into how you use these utensils as you experiment in the kitchen. Imagine the knife not just slicing through vegetables but also cutting through obstacles. Stir your cauldron of soup with the intent of stirring in positivity and nourishment. Through this simple yet powerful act, you align the ordinary with the extraordinary.

A mortar and pestle, ordinarily used for crushing spices and herbs, becomes an indispensable tool for the alchemist in the Kitchen Witch's routine.

A besom (or broom) symbolizes sweeping away negative energy and creating a sacred space. It serves a purpose beyond cleaning the house: In the realm of magic, it symbolizes the act of sweeping away negativity and creating a sacred space. Take a few moments before beginning any magical work to symbolically sweep away any energetic debris with your besom. This will create a clean slate on which to cast your spells and perform your rituals.

While a cauldron adds a touch of whimsy and mystery to your kitchen, it's essential to note that it's not a prerequisite for practicing Kitchen Witchcraft. Your everyday pots and pans can serve the same purpose with a sprinkle of intention. Bless and set the intention before use. The essence lies not in the tool itself but in the mindful infusion of your craft.

Spells and Rituals

As a Kitchen Witch knows, not all spells need incantations. For these witches, the intention is more powerful than anything else. The key to effective rituals is to infuse every action with mindfulness and intention.

The use of spells and rituals has been a longstanding tradition in many cultures, often serving as a means to manifest intentions and bring about positive change. A favorite of the Kitchen Witch is a cinnamon blessing ritual to cleanse and protect their home.

Note: Check out the "Witchy Products" page at the back of this book for a magical shopping experience, providing all the essential items and ingredients for your spells and rituals.

New Month Ritual

What you will need:

- A handful of ground cinnamon

Incantation

In this sacred space, I release what no longer serves,

As the spice ignites, negativity takes flight,

Transformed to light, I welcome the positive and bright.

Instructions

1. Sweep out your space, getting into all the nooks and crannies. You can use a special besom or a regular broom. If you are more technologically inclined, you can let your little Roomba friend do the heavy lifting. Just be sure to clean out the filters and collection chamber.

2. Gather your handful of cinnamon and stand at the threshold of your front door or the main entrance to your home.

3. Face your home, as if you are being invited in.

4. Set your intention for prosperity, protection, and good luck.

5. Speak your incantation out loud, embodying the energy.

6. When you are ready, blow the cinnamon into your home, over the threshold, inviting the energy in.

7. You can do this ritual on the first day of every new month.

Kitchen Witch Protection Simmer Pot

A note: Please don't leave your simmer pots unattended.

What you will need:

- 4 cups of moon water
- 1 cinnamon stick
- 1 tbsp dried rosemary
- 1 tbsp dried thyme

- 1 tbsp whole cloves
- A pinch of salt
- A black tourmaline or hematite crystal

Instructions

1. In a pot, combine the water, cinnamon stick, dried rosemary, dried thyme, and whole cloves.

2. Add a pinch of salt to the mixture.

3. Place the pot on the stove and turn the heat to low.

4. As the water begins to warm, focus on your intentions of protection and joy. Visualize a shield of positive energy surrounding your space.

5. Once the water starts to simmer, let the delightful aroma of cinnamon and cloves fill the air.

6. You can leave it simmering for an hour (or more, if you want to), but remember to keep an eye on it to prevent complete evaporation and a fire hazard.

7. For a little extra witchy magic: When you are done, and once the simmer pot has cooled completely, you can strain out the liquid and pour it into a spray bottle. Use this to take your protection spell with you or to refresh your space!

Morning Coffee Manifestation

What you will need:

- Your favorite coffee (home-brewed, Starbucks, or even instant coffee will do)
- Sweetener of your choice

- Milk or cream (optional)
- A spoon for stirring
- Your favorite mug

Instructions

1. Brew your coffee as you normally would, or grab a cup from your favorite coffee shop.

2. As your coffee is brewing, take a moment to clear your mind. Focus on the specific manifestation or goal you want to achieve. Whether it's attracting positivity, success, or specific opportunities, be clear about your intention.

3. Imagine your desired outcome manifesting as you pour your coffee into your favorite mug. If you got your favorite drink order from your local coffee shop, imagine your outcome manifesting as you prepare to add the extras.

4. Reinforce your desired outcome as you add sweetener, cream, or any other extras. If you take your coffee black, then proceed to the next step.

5. As you stir your coffee, visualize the energy you want to attract swirling within the cup. For manifestation, it's important to stir clockwise to *bring things in*.

6. Enjoy your coffee in your favorite place.

Orange and Vanilla Self-Love Syrup

What you will need:

- Peel of one orange (no pith)
- Juice of one orange

- 1/2 cup sugar
- Water
- Stove top
- Saucepan
- 1/4 tsp vanilla extract
- A few drops of orange blossom essence, or 1 tbsp dried orange blossoms

Incantation

In my sacred space I stand,

A witch of warmth, with spell in hand.

Orange, vibrant, symbol of zest,

Sugar, sweet, self-love manifest.

Stirring clockwise, intentions clear,

Self-love blooms, drawing near.

As sugar sweetens, so shall I,

In the mirror of my soul, I fly.

With gratitude and love, so be,

This spell is cast, blessed be.

Instructions

1. Take one orange and peel it. Gently scrape the pith (that bitter white stuff) away. Slice the peel into thin strips and set

aside.

2.   Juice the orange after you have peeled it, and strain.

3.   In a saucepan, add the sugar.

4.   Add the orange juice to a half cup, then fill the remainder with water until you have a combined half cup of liquid.

5.   Add the orange peel and vanilla extract.

6.   Over medium heat, stir until bubbles form, then lower the heat to an almost simmer while reciting the incantation above.

7.   Stir occasionally while you let it simmer down for about 10–15 minutes, then remove from the heat. Add your drops of essence or your dried blossoms. Let it cool at room temperature and allow to rest for at least 30 minutes.

8.   Once it has completely cooled, you can strain your syrup into a pretty glass bottle of your choice and refrigerate.

*****

After experimenting with these spells, feel free to explore other witchcraft types that capture your interest. Don't forget to read the Conclusion, especially if you're not reading the book sequentially.

Keep an eye out for an upcoming book dedicated to Kitchen Witchcraft! Join the email list and receive a free spell (just visit the link below or scan the QR code on the next page).

https://www.unleashingyourinnerwitch.com/get-notified

Chapter 8:

Hedge Witchery–Traversing Realms
Beyond Our Own

Whether you were led here by the quiz or by your own natural curiosity, allow yourself to be fully absorbed into this chapter on Hedge Witchcraft. If, by the end, you feel a profound connection resonating within, then you've unearthed your magical path. If not, venture forth into the exploration of other types to uncover the one that aligns more closely with your spirit.

An Overview

While there is some overlap between Hedge Witchcraft and Green Witchcraft, they are distinct practices. Herbs and plants play an important role in magical rituals in both traditions, which emphasize a strong bond with nature. Having said that, the two practices have different focal points and emphases.

The practice of Hedge Witchcraft, often associated with "hedge riding" or "journeying," requires the witch to traverse the thresholds between this world and the next, where darkness and light coexist. Those of us who practice Hedge Witchcraft are skilled in the exploration of the boundaries of consciousness, communication with spirits, and reaching out to dimensions that are not of this world.

Hedge Witches often do what is known as "astral travel" or journeying, which entails deliberately disentangling themselves from their physical bodies in order to explore other spiritual dimensions. Meditation, trances, or guided visualizations could be part of this process. And it is of utmost importance to focus on spiritual protection during these journeys.

The "hedge" is a representation of the distance that separates the visible and the invisible. Think of the in-between spaces like doorways—the moment between night and morning. It all represents the hedge or boundary of the world around us.

In order to gain access to wisdom, guidance, and energies that are beyond the realm of the physical, Hedge Witches are able to deftly cross this threshold and enter a state of altered consciousness.

As part of Hedge Witchcraft rituals, it is usual practice to connect with spirit guides, who are entities from other dimensions that aid with direction, protection, and insight while traveling through the astral plane. The belief that there are multiple dimensions and realities beyond our own is something that Hedge Witches embrace. The Hedge Witch considers the hedge to be a gateway to these different realms, each of which contains energy, entities, and knowledge that are distinct from the others.

Hedge Witches believe that the spiritual and physical worlds are inextricably linked. They frequently interpret the coincidences, omens, and signs they see as messages from the afterlife, which helps them on their journeys.

Witches who practice in this way frequently create sacred spaces (more on that in a bit), whether those spaces are physical or metaphysical, in which they experience a powerful connection to the spiritual realms. Astral travel and communion with energies from other worlds are both possible through these spaces, which serve as gateways.

During these rituals, the mind and spirit are prepared for astral travel through the use of various techniques. This may involve chanting, meditation, or the utilization of particular tools and symbols in order to strengthen the connection to the unseen.

Hedge Witches are able to return from their astral travels with knowledge, insights, and energies that they have gained from other realms, which they then apply to their everyday lives, integrating these experiences into their magical practices and fostering personal growth.

Those individuals who are interested in going beyond the confines of the familiar and discovering the realms that lie beyond the hedge are encouraged to engage in Hedge Witchery. Hedge Witches navigate the liminal spaces with bravery and curiosity, thereby revealing the mysteries that lie just beyond our everyday perception, dancing between the seen and the unseen.

Astral Travel

The capacity to astral travel, journey, or ride the hedges is a hallmark of Hedge Witchcraft that allows its practitioners to access these other dimensions. In this sense, "traveling" means that the practitioner's awareness leaves the physical body in order to investigate other realms, establish communication with the spirit world, or acquire new understandings.

Because of the inherent dangers of traversing the spiritual realms, hedge riding safety is of the utmost importance. Before setting out on such journeys, Hedge Witches often stress the importance of being well-prepared, protected, and grounded. Protective amulets, visualization techniques, or spirit guides are some of the tools they may use to keep things under control. Hedge Witches, like practitioners of any magic, must engage with the unseen in a responsible and courteous manner.

Setting Up Your Space

Setting up your magical space involves creating a harmonious balance between the natural world and the spirit world. It needs to allow a connection and exchange between yourself and the spirits you work with.

Setting Up Your Sacred Space

Find somewhere peaceful and undisturbed, whether that is inside or out.

Build your altar on a level surface, such as a table or a shelf. Cover it with a cloth made of natural materials such as cotton or linen, adding an earthy touch.

Add sentimental objects, such as crystals, charms, or trinkets, to imbue it with your own energy. Align your practice with your belief system by incorporating spiritual symbols like runes, sigils, or representations of deities. By leaving offerings that have significance for the divine or the spirits, you can acknowledge your connection with them.

Candles play a crucial role in Hedge Witchcraft—select colors based on their magical associations or the energies you wish to invoke (should you need some guidance here, the Glossary breaks this down for you).

Setting up your altar is a deeply personal and intuitive process that reflects your unique connection with the energies you work with. There is no wrong way to do this.

Tools of the Hedge Witch

Hedge Witches have a wide variety of tools at their disposal. The pendulum moves with energy, unraveling insights through subtle motions. Spirit bottles, laden with protective herbs, stand guard against negativity. A black scrying mirror unveils messages from the spirit realm. Mirrors help them look within, while tarot cards or runes can help them make sense of their past, present, and future. These magical implements, when used in tandem, give the Hedge Witch a formidable arsenal.

Black Scrying Mirror

This is an important tool you can use to connect with your intuition or access spiritual guidance, and it is often used in reflection rituals or psychic vision spells. You can also combine this scrying tool with the "Second Sight Tea" spell below.

What you will need:

- Picture frame with glass (preferably without any beveling)
- Acrylic paint or spray paint in a matte black finish
- Brush for painting
- Protective covering or newspaper to cover your work surface
- Mild soap and water
- Paper towels or a soft cloth that won't scratch the glass surface

Instructions

1. **Pick out a frame:** Pick out a picture frame that has a glass front. If you want a smooth scrying surface, beveled glass is not the way to go.

2. **Prepare the workspace and be aware of personal safety:** To protect surfaces from paint, cover your work area with newspaper or another protective covering. Use spray paint only in well-ventilated areas and wear a ventilator mask or N95 mask. Eye protection is also a good idea. Follow the instructions on the items you will be using.

3. **Clean the glass:** The glass pane can be easily cleaned with a little mild soap and lukewarm water. Remove any fingerprints, dirt, or dust to ensure a smooth painting surface.

4. **Apply paint:** If using spray paint, evenly coat only one side of the glass with the black matte spray paint. Following the manufacturer's instructions, apply light, even coats. Allow each coat to dry before applying the next. If you are using acrylic paint, mix it with water to create a slightly diluted consistency. This helps apply it in an even coat. Apply the paint evenly with a brush, covering the entire glass surface. Allow it to dry completely. Keep adding coats until the

surface is completely black. The goal is to create an opaque background that minimizes reflections.

5. **Let it dry:** Allow the paint to dry completely. The paint used will determine how long this might take. Hold the glass up to the light to ensure the black surface is uniform and free from streaks or uneven patches.

6. **Reassemble the frame:** Once the paint is fully dry and you're satisfied with the results, reassemble the frame. Flip the glass around to ensure the painted side is facing inward to protect the paint and give you an even smoother surface to work with.

7. **Charge and dedicate:** State your intentions clearly, dedicate your mirror for scrying, and add it to your divination practice.

8. **Storage:** When it's not in use, store your scrying mirror in a safe place. You can wrap it in a soft scarf or cloth to prevent scratches or damage to your tool.

Spells and Rituals

Note: Check out the "Witchy Products" page at the back of this book for a magical shopping experience, providing all the essential items and ingredients for your spells and rituals.

Starting with a protection spell is of utmost importance when working with the magical energies of the world around you—and even more so when it comes to Hedge Witchcraft, which is why the first spell is a powerful protection spell. This one will require a protection sigil, so do be sure to have one ready (you can check out Chapter 9 for more on sigils).

Astral Travel Protection Spell

What you will need:

- Small fabric sachet or pouch
- 1 tsp dried rosemary
- 1 tsp dried basil
- 1 tsp dried lavender
- 2–3 bay leaves
- Black tourmaline crystal
- Sharpie or marker

Instructions

1. Fill the sachet with your chosen mixture of herbs, except the bay leaves.

2. Add the small black tourmaline crystal to the sachet.

3. Before placing the bay leaves in the sachet, you have the option of either writing your intention for protection on them or visualizing it while holding them in your palm. If you have created a protection sigil (see Chapter 9 or the Glossary), you can draw that upon the bay leaves before adding them to the sachet.

4. To close the sachet, pull the drawstrings tightly. Alternately, concentrate on the goal of protection as you seal the sachet however you see fit.

5. Carry the sachet with you or place it on the edge of your altar for astral protection during your rituals.

6. Recharge the sachet by placing it in direct sunlight or a full

moon once a month.

Spirit Guide Invocation Spell

What you will need:

- Lavender oil or incense
- Clear quartz crystal
- Blue or white candle, placed in a holder or fireproof dish
- An offering such as herbs, flowers, or a small treat

Incantation

Spirit guides, guardians unseen,

Join me beyond the hedge and share your wisdom.

Through the veil that separates realms,

I call upon your presence, ancient and divine.

By the power of hedge and crossroads bound,

Let our energies seamlessly resound.

In this sacred space where realms converge,

Grant me insight, let wisdom surge.

Instructions

1. Diffuse a few drops of lavender oil into a tealight or light lavender incense in an incense holder and let the aroma fill the room.

2. Hold the transparent quartz crystal in your hands and visualize its link to the ethereal realms. When you are ready, set it in the middle of your altar or sacred space.

3. Now light the blue or white candle, stating your intention or repeating the incantation.

4. Sit quietly, breathing deeply, and visualize a serene landscape beyond the hedge.

5. Invite your spirit guides to communicate with you and share their wisdom.

6. Put a little token of your appreciation near the crystal as an offering. Here you can offer whatever it is that you feel a connection to, whether it be a deity, spirit guides, or something else entirely. (I like to use chocolate, not only because it is a sweet treat, but cacao has grounding properties that will keep you from getting swept away.)

7. Listen to any insights or messages that come to you.

8. After you have finished, give thanks to your ancestors and put out the candle. You can let the incense or oil burn until it burns out completely or until the oil evaporates. Do not leave your candles unattended.

Second Sight Tea

This is a potent tea that makes enough brew for two to three cups. Please consult your medical professional before drinking it, as some medications can have adverse effects when combined with certain herbs.

What you will need:

- Teapot
- 1 tsp dried mugwort
- 1 tsp dried lavender
- 1 tsp dried chamomile
- 1 tsp dried lemon balm
- Honey to taste

Incantation

In the mystic realm where visions lay,

With tea in hand, I find my way.

Brew of herbs and leaves so bright,

Open my eyes to second sight.

Instructions

1. Gather all of your dried herbs and mix them together. You can store these in an airtight jar if you want to make the tea in bulk.

2. Arrange the teapot in its designated spot and, if it has a strainer basket, place the herbs inside it. Otherwise, just place your herbs at the base of your teapot.

3. Pour boiling water over the herbs.

4. Depending on how strong you want your tea, let the herbs steep for 5–10 minutes.

5. Before adding honey, strain the herbs if necessary.

6. Stir clockwise, focusing your intent on enhancing your

intuitive abilities and receiving clear visions.

Meditation

Note before you begin: Keep a notebook and pen close by to write down anything you feel called to. For the more technologically inclined, you can use the "notes" app on your phone or another device.

1. Find a quiet and comfortable space.

2. Gently cup the hot tea between your palms and enjoy its comforting warmth.

3. Center yourself by taking a few deep breaths, and let the warmth pass through you.

4. Imagine yourself encircled by a gentle, indigo light that acts as a shield.

5. Drink the tea slowly, savoring each sip as you taste it and feel its warmth.

6. Recite your incantation.

7. As you sip, allow your mind to enter a state of calm and receptivity.

8. Focus on your breath as it flows in and out of you, letting go of any tension or distractions.

9. Allow your thoughts to flow without judgment.

10. Embrace any visions or insights that come to you. You can write them down at the end of your meditation or as they come up.

11. When you feel your meditation is complete, express gratitude to your guides for their protection and for the new insights you have gained.

*****

As you close this chapter, keep the Glossary in mind—a treasure trove of wisdom awaits your exploration and understanding.

Once you've worked through the spells above, I invite you to venture into other witchcraft types that appeal to you. Make sure to read the Conclusion, even if you're not reading each chapter in order.

There is also an upcoming book focusing on Hedge Witchcraft (and other related titles), so be sure to sign up to the email list by entering the link below into your browser or scanning the QR code (you also get a free spell when you do!).

https://www.unleashingyourinnerwitch.com/get-notified

Chapter 9:

Chaos Magick–Embracing Uncertainty and Unpredictability

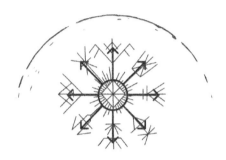

Whether, in your chaotic brilliance, you decided to simply jump to a random chapter and landed here, or you were guided by your results from the quiz, let's dive into the heart of Chaos Magick.

Very often, things happen in life that just feel completely chaotic.

Out of our seeming control.

And yet, there are those witches who thrive in this chaos. To those rare few who embrace the discord and turn it to their will, chaos is one of the most powerful tools in their magical arsenal.

This is simply because, rooted in the philosophy that *belief itself* is a potent magical tool, these witches thrive in the ever-shifting landscape of uncertainty.

If chaos is where your magic thrives, then this chapter is yours to explore. Whether by quiz or by fate, dive into the ever-shifting landscape of uncertainty and embrace the potency chaos brings to your magical journey.

An Overview

One of the distinguishing characteristics of Chaos Magick (other than it is almost always spelled "magick" rather than "magic") is a dynamic approach that places a strong emphasis on personal experimentation, absurdity, and—most importantly—adaptability.

Chaos Witches embrace the concept that belief is a tool—one that can be adopted, discarded, or modified at will. There is a strong emphasis on practicality, on picking beliefs that help with the current magical task at hand. They are masters of paradigm-shifting, able to effortlessly switch between various magical frameworks or belief systems depending on the circumstances. This fluidity allows them to draw from a diverse range of traditions and practices and root them in their sigil magic.

Sigil magic is a hallmark of Chaos Magick. In order for the magic to operate on a deeper level, practitioners frequently forget the specifics when they release the symbols (sigils) they have created to symbolize their desires into the subconscious or the universe.

To unleash their full magical potential, Chaos Witches welcome uncertainty.

The unpredictability of reality is viewed as an opportunity for imaginative and fantastical exploration and creation, rather than as a limitation.

Chaos Magick breaks down inflexible belief systems and dogma. Chaos Witches do not adhere rigidly to any one pantheon or tradition, but rather, they experiment with different ways of thinking to find what works best for their magical practices. Meditation, trance, or other techniques that alter perception and make the mind susceptible to magical influence may be used for this purpose.

Chaos Magick, which is both dynamic and liberating, flourishes in the disorder of uncertainty. Embracing unpredictability as a source of power, Chaos Witches live on the edges of belief, conjuring spells that reflect the ever-shifting nature of reality and embracing change.

Setting Up Your Space

While the limitless energy of chaos is essential to your craft as a witch in this tradition, your sacred space does not have to reflect that chaos. Imagine your altar as a reflective surface for the dynamic and unpredictable forces you control, a place for "controlled chaos" to unfold.

To set up your altar, you'll need a sturdy surface like a shelf or a desk in a quiet and private space. Lay a dark-colored or black fabric down as a basis to symbolize the void or chaos from which all creation emerges. Add any items that symbolize your connection to chaos. This can be anything from a cracked eggshell to a personal object that has meaning and value to you. You can also add candles of any color—you can even explore the aspects of all the colors if you so desire. Follow your intuition.

Whatever your style may be—organized chaos or full-on chaos—the most important thing is to make it uniquely yours. Remember that reverence and disorder can coexist, and try to keep your space clean even in the midst of all the mayhem. Your altar, like your craft, deserves respect, even within the realm of chaos.

Sigils

Note: Check out the "Witchy Products" page at the back of this book for a magical shopping experience, providing all the essential items and ingredients for your spells and rituals.

Since Chaos Magick is powered by sigils, let's begin by breaking down what they are and how you can make your own.

You can represent specific intentions, desires, or outcomes with sigils, which are magical symbols. A number of magical traditions make use of them, including Chaos Witchcraft, to help concentrate and strengthen the practitioner's will. Condensing a declaration of purpose into an abstract symbol is what sigil creation is all about:

1. **Set your intention:** Clearly define the intention or desire for which you want to create the sigil. Be specific and concise in formulating your statement.

2. **Condense your statement:** Condense your statement into a few key words. Remove vowels and duplicate consonants. Let's say your intention is "Embrace change for transformation." The condensed form might be "MBRCHNGFTRNSFRMN."

3. **Create a design:** Make an abstract design using the condensed letters. Combine and modify the letters into a unique symbol. Be creative and let your intuition guide you. The final pattern does not need to resemble any of the initial letters. What is important is that the symbol stands out visually and conveys your intention clearly.

A number of free sigil creation tools are available online to help you out if the idea of making your own symbol is too daunting. As soon as you input your intention, the computer will take care of everything else. Then it's a simple matter of printing your sigil to use in your spell! You can also trace it with tracing paper and a pencil or draw it freehand.

4. **Charge the sigil:** Charge the sigil with your energy and intention. This can be done through meditation, visualization, or incorporating it into a ritual. The idea is to infuse the sigil with your focused intent.

5. **Release the energy:** Once charged, release the energy by activating the sigil. This can be achieved through burning the sigil or incorporating it into a spell or ritual.

Spells

Chaos Witchcraft utilizes sigils more frequently than the other types and chooses sigils over incantations. In the spells below, I have replaced them with "power words" that can be condensed to suit the specific sigil and spell.

Crafting personalized sigils that capture the essence of your intentions is built upon these significant and concise phrases. By incorporating your goals into your spells, as a Chaos Witch you can harness the dynamic and ever-changing nature of chaos to achieve your goals.

The sigils that correspond to the power words gain the raw power of chaos from the concentrated magical effects of the words. This deviation from conventional spellcasting highlights the adaptability inherent in Chaos Witchcraft.

While you can draw your sigil on any surface, most spells require the sigil to be burned, so drawing it on paper is the most effective way to incorporate it into your spellwork.

Special note: Laughter is a wonderful tool to use to end any spell or ritual in Chaos Magick, since it can dissipate any remaining psychic energy or lurking entities that may remain.

Chaos Shield

What you will need:

- Black candle
- Dragon's blood incense
- Small mirror
- Sigil
- Fireproof bowl

Power word or phrase

Chaos be my guard.

Instructions

1. Set the small mirror in the center of your altar.

2. Place the incense and candle inside the fireproof bowl, in any order you wish, and light them both.

3. Allow a few moments for the smoke to permeate the space.

4. Place the sigil on top of the mirror.

5. When you are ready, gaze into the mirror, embracing chaos.

6. Repeat your power word or phrase as you gaze into the mirror.

7. Light the sigil on fire using the candle and let it burn to ash in the bowl.

8. You can let the candle burn down or extinguish it safely. Keep the ashes on your altar until your next spell.

Chaos Infusion Spell

This spell seeks to channel chaotic forces for unpredictable and powerful outcomes by using a white candle, ashes from previous chaotic workings, and a specially crafted oil that is infused with chaos. The goal is to let go of control and let chaos be the catalyst that creates new opportunities.

What you will need:

- A white candle
- Ashes (collected from a previous chaotic working)
- Chaos oil (blend of equal parts patchouli, bergamot, and clove oils together)
- Sigil
- Fireproof bowl

Power word or phrase

Chaos unfolds.

Instructions

1. Take a few moments to center yourself, connecting with the chaotic forces you aim to invoke. Feel the energy building

around you.

2. Anoint the candle in the oil and roll it in the ashes.

3. Put the candle on top of the sigil, inside your fireproof bowl.

4. Focus on your intention of harnessing the energies of chaos.

5. Light the candle.

6. Focus on the flame, embracing the unpredictable nature of chaos.

7. Visualize the energies swirling around you, breaking down barriers and opening doors to new possibilities.

8. Let the candle burn completely, releasing the chaos-infused energy into the universe.

Impulsive Luck Infusion Spell

What you will need:

- A small object (a coin, key, or trinket)
- A marker (to draw your sigil onto the small object)
- A pinch of salt
- A red candle, placed in a holder or fireproof dish

Power word or phrase

Fortune's chaos weave your thread.

Instruction

1. Sprinkle a pinch of salt over your object of choice. Salt is associated with purification and protection, ensuring that the luck attracted is positive and beneficial.

2. Using the marker, draw your sigil on your object.

3. Hold the object in your hands and focus on the intention of attracting good luck through chaotic and unpredictable means. Envision random, fortunate events manifesting in your life.

4. Light the red candle and let it burn for a moment, observing the dance of the flame.

5. Hold the object above the flame of the candle for a few seconds, allowing the heat to infuse it with those wild energies.

6. Allow the candle to burn for a few more moments and extinguish it safely.

*****

I encourage you to delve into other witchcraft types that resonate with you once you have worked your way through these spells. Don't forget to check out the Conclusion regardless of the order you are reading these chapters in! Oh, and sign up to the email list (entering the link below into your browser or scanning the QR code below) to be one of the first to be notified when a new book gets released (you also get a free Chaos spell when you do).

https://www.unleashingyourinnerwitch.com/get-notified

Chapter 10:

Eclectic Witchcraft–Creating a Personalized Path

At the core of Eclectic Witchcraft lie intuition and adaptability. Whether you've arrived here by quiz or your own intuitive inner magic, welcome to your one-of-a-kind spiritual adventure as you discover, modify, and develop your own magical practices.

An Overview

By drawing inspiration from a diverse range of traditions, cultures, and personal experiences, Eclectic Witchcraft is a method of practicing magic that is both fluid and inclusive.

It is not uncommon for Eclectic Witches to effortlessly incorporate practices and beliefs from a variety of different traditions, whether it be aspects of Wicca, Traditional Witchcraft—or any of the other witchcraft types covered in this book—or another system that speaks to them. Their individual journey is reflected in the final product, which is a well-balanced combination.

Individualizing rituals and spells in accordance with specific needs and preferences is a common practice. In the realm of Eclectic Magic, there are no strict guidelines to follow; rather, the outcomes of these magical works are as diverse as the practitioner's influences and intentions themselves.

Eclectic Witches create their own system of symbolism and draw upon magical and ancestral traditions, while also incorporating personal symbols, colors, and associations that have profound meaning to them into their magical practices.

The pursuit of individual spiritual exploration is of utmost importance for them. It is more important to pursue and embrace what resonates within their own experiences, insights, and inner truths than it is to blindly follow a set of beliefs that have been predetermined by any one witch that came before.

Eclectic Witchcraft is based on the principles of openness and acceptance, of old traditions and new thoughts.

By showing respect for the beliefs of others and recognizing the variety of magical practices, those who practice this type of magic are able to cultivate a community that recognizes and appreciates the many different ways in which individuals choose to live their lives.

You are afforded the opportunity to investigate the vast and varied landscape of magical worlds when you engage in the practice of Eclectic Magic. You are not only urged to pursue your passions and trust your intuition, but also empowered to forge a path as diverse and multifaceted as you are. Your passions and intuition aren't just acknowledged—they are celebrated and nurtured.

The charm of celebrating special times of the year in the Eclectic Witchcraft tradition lies in incorporating parts of many different cultures' festivities with your own unique customs and practices. By purposefully combining elements from different sources, you can add depth to the occasion and find inspiration in unexpected places. Personalizing the celebrations associated with the Wheel of the Year and lunar cycles is a prevalent practice, creating a deep sense of connection with the craft.

Through the incorporation of your one-of-a-kind energy and personal touch into these moments, you are able to amplify the magic, thereby cultivating a profound and meaningful connection with natural cycles and the spiritual essence of the craft.

No other witch possesses magic as uniquely tailored to you, making every spell, incantation, and ritual a manifestation of your singular and extraordinary connection to the mystical.

Setting Up Your Space

When it comes to Eclectic Witchcraft, it is common for practitioners to create spaces that represent the different facets of their practice. The materials used to build altars are often rather *eclectic* (see what I did there?). These materials vary from person to person, practice to practice, and contain a variety of objects, from personal items and artifacts from different cultures to symbols that are meaningful to each individual.

Creating a sacred and personalized space for your practice involves a thoughtful arrangement of items on your altar. Trusting your intuition is key, allowing you to adapt and customize your space based on what resonates with you.

Establish a central focal point by introducing an item of personal significance—whether a cherished crystal, a meaningful statue, or a symbol exemplifying your spiritual journey. Incorporate these symbolic representations from your eclectic path—from sacred shapes, symbols, and runes—around this focal point, making sure to select each one for its personal resonance.

As you arrange these items on your altar, let your intuition guide you, ensuring that the layout exudes energetic balance and alignment. Create a one-of-a-kind sacred sanctuary that is uniquely yours by adding sentimental objects like a cherished piece of jewelry, a keepsake from a bygone era, or a written intention that imbues the entirety of your unique energy. Gather items for your altar that speak to your spiritual journey, and let your intuition guide you as you do so.

Spells

The practice of Eclectic Witchcraft opens up a world of limitless creativity, especially when it comes to spells. This form of magic invites you to tap into the vast well of your intuition, creating spells that effortlessly meld various styles and methods from different traditions, and adding your unique touch to them.

The beauty of eclectic magic lies in adaptability, allowing you to tailor spells to suit your unique desires, preferences, and spiritual inclinations. While it encourages you to explore, keep in mind the different aspects of herbs, crystals, and other magical components.

After you've delved into the spells, think about trying your hand at other forms of witchcraft that draw your interest. Read the Conclusion, even if you aren't reading the book in order.

Note: Check out the "Witchy Products" page at the back of this book for a magical shopping experience, providing all the essential items and ingredients for your spells and rituals.

Protection Charm Pouch

What you will need:

- Small, breathable mesh or organza pouch
- 1 tsp dried basil
- 1 tsp dried rosemary
- 1 tsp dried mint
- Half a stick of cinnamon
- 1 bay leaf
- Small black tourmaline crystal
- Marker

Incantation

Ward against what's left unseen.

Instructions

1. Take a moment to center yourself.
2. On the bay leaf, write the incantation in marker.
3. Hold the tourmaline between your palms, visualizing a shield of protective energy forming around you.
4. Add the crystal to the pouch.
5. Add the basil, rosemary, mint, and cinnamon to the pouch.

6. As you add the bay leaf, repeat the incantation, visualizing its power enveloping and radiating out from you.

7. Pull the drawstrings to seal the pouch and close the ritual, taking a moment to sit in the stillness of the moment.

8. Keep the protection charm bag with you, whether in your pocket, purse, or hanging from a necklace.

Health and Vitality Spell

What you will need:

- A small clear quartz crystal
- Fresh eucalyptus leaves
- Fresh lavender sprigs
- A small piece of amethyst
- A white candle, placed in a holder or fireproof dish
- A small jar with a lid
- Coarse salt
- Salt water for cleansing (optional)

Incantation

Clear crystal, amplify my intent,

Healing energies and wishes sent.

Eucalyptus, bring health my way,

Lavender, peace in every day.

Amethyst, stone of divine grace,

Bring healing energies to this space.

Instructions

1. Begin by purifying your space. This can be done through your own personal methods, or by lighting incense and allowing the smoke to drift through the space.

2. Light the white candle.

3. Start your ritual by passing the clear crystal through the smoke of the candle and reciting the first two lines of the incantation.

4. Hold the clear quartz and focus on your intention for healing and wish fulfillment. Visualize yourself or whomever the spell is for in perfect health, and see your wish come true.

5. Fill the jar with the lavender sprigs and eucalyptus leaves and recite the next two lines of the incantation.

6. Place the clear quartz crystal into the jar, along with the tiny amethyst, while saying the final two lines of the incantation and allowing the healing energies to permeate your surroundings.

7. Focus on the flame of the candle, concentrating on your wish, visualizing it, and manifesting it. Feel the comforting heat of the candle, a symbol of the healing energy surrounding you or your person.

8. Once you have added the coarse salt, seal the jar tightly.

9. Give the candle some time to burn. Once the candle has burned for a short time, extinguish it and let the wax drip onto the jar's lid. With this, your intention is sealed into the

jar.

10. Dip your fingers in the salt water and flick droplets around the jar as well as your space, repeating this intention: "Salt, purify and protect, seal the spell, my will direct."

11. Put the jar somewhere you will see it every day to serve as a visual reminder of your wish and intention.

Hidden Truths Revealed Spell

In the witchcraft community, disagreements often arise over ethical considerations related to spells. You will find this spell, which is meant to reveal hidden truths, particularly useful when you feel that someone is hiding something or is harboring malicious intentions.

Since the spell explores the domain of unveiling things that may have been purposefully concealed from you, it is essential to approach this practice with awareness and a thorough understanding of the possible effects on other people. Treat others with dignity and respect as you use your magical abilities, and never compromise on ethics. The goal here is not to cause harm, but to clear the air and expose hidden truths.

Be aware, some truths might be hard for you to accept, so be sure you really want to know.

What you will need:

- Purple candle
- Bay leaves, crushed
- Ground cinnamon
- Clear quartz crystal
- Sea salt

- Small mirror

- Fireproof bowl

- Pen and paper

Incantation

Mirror, mirror, reveal what's concealed,

Hidden truths now stand revealed.

As above, so below,

Secrets exposed, the truth now shown.

Instructions

1. Prepare your space. Choose a quiet area to ensure you won't be interrupted during the ritual.

2. In the fireproof bowl, mix the cinnamon, bay leaves, and a pinch of sea salt. Place the bowl in the center of your workspace.

3. Place the purple candle in the bowl, ensuring it cannot tip over. Place the small mirror in front of it, facing you.

4. While you are holding the quartz crystal in your hands, concentrate on the outcome of the spell as well as the intention you have for it. Place the crystal in front of the mirror.

5. On the paper, write down what you seek to uncover or reveal. Be specific about the hidden truths you want to come to light.

6. Light the purple candle, focusing on the flame.

7. Gaze into the mirror and repeat your incantation, holding the paper in your left hand.

8. Light the paper with the candle flame and let it burn in the fireproof bowl along with the herbs, thus activating their essences and transmuting their energies. As the paper burns, visualize the hidden truths being exposed.

9. Close out your spell by thanking the energies and elements you have called upon. Leave the candle to burn out safely.

*****

Some very exciting new books are in the works, one of which is devoted entirely to Eclectic Witchcraft. Just enter the link below into your browser or scan the QR code to receive early alerts and a free Eclectic Spell.

https://www.unleashingyourinnerwitch.com/get-notified

Conclusion

Your initiation into the realm of witchcraft marks a significant milestone. Your commitment, regardless of whether you have only scratched the surface or explored every possible facet, is indicative of your growing knowledge and natural inquisitiveness. May the closing of this chapter not mark its end but the beginning of even greater illumination and miraculous discovery.

As a practitioner of magic, you will discover your own individual path within the expansive and captivating world of witchcraft. Along the way, you will encounter a wide variety of spells, rituals, and tools, all of which are directed by your intuition and your intentions.

Take stock of how far you have come as a witch as you contemplate your exploration of the many witchcraft types. Whether you identify more with the organized rituals of Wicca, the wild anarchy of Chaos Magick, or the balanced fusion of Eclectic Witchcraft, you deserve to celebrate. Every step, every spell, and every exploration has contributed to your growth as a witch and, hopefully, as a person as well.

Embrace the path you've embarked upon, knowing that each twist and turn in the road unveils opportunities for growth and wonder. Revel in the knowledge gained and the accomplishments achieved, for they are stepping stones on your magical path. Admire the majesty and scope of witchcraft as it reflects your own boundless possibilities.

Keep in mind that getting there is half the fun, and that every curve in the road will bring new opportunities for growth and wonder.

The knowledge you have received and the things you have accomplished are stepping stones on your enchanted path—celebrate them.

Conjuring Knowledge: Expanding What You Know Beyond Beginner Level

Consider the exciting opportunities that lie ahead for your ongoing development and the expansion of your knowledge in the field of witchcraft as you move from the beginner's stage to a more advanced level. The journey ahead is full of exciting chances to learn more about magic and get better at using it. As a witch, your path is always an adventure of discovery and growth, so enjoy learning new things and traveling to new places.

As you explore more profound aspects of the traditions that speak to you, immerse yourself in more advanced magical practices and seek knowledge from a wide variety of sources. Attend workshops, join covens or online communities, and engage in meaningful discussions with fellow practitioners. Keep in mind that the path of a witch is one that is constantly changing and that the pursuit of knowledge is a venture that lasts a lifetime. Take pleasure in the process of discovery and allow your hunger for knowledge to lead you to uncharted territories within the realm of the craft.

Throughout these chapters, you were able to delve into each of the seven different types of witchcraft covered in this book. To aid in your continued education, there is more to come in the *Unleashing Your Inner Witch* series, with books in the works solely dedicated to each type of witchcraft as well as companion journals. If you haven't already, I invite you to sign up for our email list to be the first to know when these books and journals are released (as well as get a free spell!) by clicking the link at the end of this chapter. Alternatively, if you are reading this in hardcover or paperback, enter the link in your browser or simply scan the QR code.

Embracing Your Journey

It is important to remember that magic is not only in the rituals you perform but also in the everyday moments when you connect with the energies that are all around you. Embrace the ups and downs that occur along your spiritual path.

Honor the sacred journey you have set out on, cultivate a sense of wonder, and keep an open mind to the possibility of new experiences. For you, I hope that each day is filled to the brim with enchantment, that your heart is filled to the brim with gratitude, and that your spirit takes on the essence of the craft.

Blessed be.

A Moment of Your Time

I would like to personally thank you for embarking on this exploration of *Unleashing Your Inner Witch* with me, and I hope you enjoyed this journey as much as I did creating it for you. Assuming so, I would be so grateful if you would be willing to share your thoughts and experience with this book by reviewing it on Amazon. It's reflections from valued readers like you that help others more easily find and enjoy this book!

To make things as easy as possible, I've provided a review link below, which you can enter manually into your browser or you may just scan the QR code below.

Thank you again and blessed be.

~Delia Raven Black

Direct Review Link for Amazon.com (U.S.):

**https://www.amazon.com/review/create-review/?
asin=B0D33N98XL**

Sign Up to Be Notified of Upcoming Releases and Get a Free Spell!

Go to the Following Link to Sign Up to Get on the Notification List and Get Your Free Bonus Spell:

https://www.unleashingyourinnerwitch.com/get-notified

Or, Simply Scan the QR Code Below:

Glossary

Here you'll find a comprehensive list of terms and concepts used throughout your magical journey. Entries are organized alphabetically for easy reference. For example, you'll find candles and their various colors listed under *"Candle, color,"* while ingredients, crystals, moon phases, and tools are grouped under their respective main topics, with individual items listed alphabetically (*"Tools, athame"* and *"Moon phases, full moon"*).

Age of Enlightenment (17th to 18th centuries): A historical period characterized by intellectual and cultural movements that emphasized reason, science, and individual rights. It marked a shift toward secularism and skepticism, influencing various areas, including philosophy, politics, and scientific inquiry.

Altar: A sacred space used for rituals, spellwork, and worship, often adorned with symbols, tools, and items of personal significance.

Anointing: The act of applying consecrated oils or magical substances to objects, tools, or oneself as a part of ritual purification or blessing.

Blessing: A ritual or spoken words intended to invoke divine favor and positive energy.

Candle, black: Banishing, protection, absorbing negative energy, breaking hexes, releasing.

Candle, blue: Communication, inspiration, wisdom, protection, tranquility.

Candle, green: Abundance, fertility, growth, healing, prosperity, luck.

Candle, pink: Love, friendship, compassion, harmony.

Candle, purple: Psychic abilities, spiritual power, wisdom, divination.

Candle, red: Love, passion, strength, courage, energy, vitality.

Candle, white: Purity, spirituality, peace, truth, cleansing, healing, protection.

Candle, yellow: Intellect, creativity, confidence, success, joy.

Casting a circle: Creating a sacred space by visualizing or physically marking a circle, often used for protection and focus during rituals.

Chaos Witchcraft: A practice that embraces chaos and unpredictability, often involving the manipulation of symbols, energies, and personal will to create change.

Charging: *See: Recharging.*

Coven: A community or group of witches who gather regularly to practice rituals, share knowledge, and support each other in their magical endeavors.

Crystals, amethyst: Associated with clarity, intuition, and spiritual awareness.

Crystals, black tourmaline: Used for grounding, protection against negative energies, and enhancing spiritual insight.

Crystals, clear quartz: Amplification.

Crystals, hematite: Grounding energy, balancing emotions, and deflecting negative energies.

Crystals, pyrite: Attracts abundance and prosperity, and enhances willpower.

Crystals, rhodonite: Promotes emotional healing, self-love, compassion, and balance.

Crystals, rose quartz: Associated with love, self-love, and emotional healing.

Crystals, tiger's eye: Enhances courage, focus, and protection.

Divination: The practice of gaining insights or foretelling the future through methods such as tarot cards, runes, scrying, or other forms of fortune telling.

Eclectic Witchcraft: A flexible and personalized approach to witchcraft, where practitioners draw inspiration and techniques from various traditions, creating their own unique path.

Esbat: A ritual or gathering held during the phases of the moon, typically focusing on lunar energy and magical workings.

Green Witchcraft: A practice that focuses on herbalism, plant magic, and a deep connection with nature. Green Witches often work with the energies of plants and the earth.

Hedge Witchcraft: A practice that involves working with the boundaries between the physical and spiritual realms, often focusing on herbalism, healing, and spirit communication.

Hermeticism: The idea that everything is interconnected, the pursuit of spiritual enlightenment, and the belief that there are universal principles that govern the universe are at the core of this movement. The phrase "as above, so below" is a reflection of the correspondence that exists between the universe and the individual.

Incantation: A recited or chanted sequence of words, often rhythmic or poetic, imbued with magical purpose.

Ingredients, aloe vera: Protection and healing.

Ingredients, basil: Love, prosperity, protection, and attracting positive energy.

Ingredients, bay leaf: Intuition and protection.

Ingredients, bergamot: Prosperity, success, and positive energy.

Ingredients, calendula: Intuition, protection, love, and psychic abilities.

Ingredients, chamomile: Peace and tranquility.

Ingredients, cinnamon: Love, protection, prosperity, and manifestation.

Ingredients, cloves: Protection and banishing.

Ingredients, coffee: Focus, motivation, and communication.

Ingredients, dill: Protection against negative energies.

Ingredients, eucalyptus: Healing and purification.

Ingredients, lavender: Relaxation, healing, and attracting positive energy.

Ingredients, lemon balm: Relaxation, happiness, and easing emotional stress.

Ingredients, mint: Healing, prosperity, and psychic abilities.

Ingredients, mugwort: Divination, dreams, enhancing psychic abilities, and facilitating astral travel.

Ingredients, orange blossom: Purity, abundance, positive energy, love, and prosperity.

Ingredients, patchouli: Love, prosperity, and grounding.

Ingredients, rose: Enhancing emotional connection and love.

Ingredients, rosemary: Protection, purification, and improved memory.

Ingredients, sage: Commonly used in smudging rituals to purify spaces and energies.

Ingredients, salt: Cleansing and protection.

Ingredients, thyme: Courage, purification, strength, and dispelling negativity.

Kitchen Witchcraft: A form of witchcraft that centers around the home and kitchen, incorporating magical practices into everyday activities like cooking and cleaning.

Lammas: A Sabbat in Wicca, celebrated on August 1st, marking the first harvest and giving thanks for the abundance of the season.

Medieval era (ca. 500–1500): A historical period marked by witch hunts and persecution of individuals accused of witchcraft. The practice of witchcraft was often associated with heresy and devil worship.

Moon phases, first quarter: Linked with overcoming challenges, taking action, and addressing obstacles in your path.

Moon phases, full moon: Associated with culmination, completion, and the height of magical power. Also for heightened intuition, clarity, and manifestation of desires.

Moon phases, last quarter: A time for evaluating progress, making adjustments, and clearing away stagnant energies.

Moon phases, new moon: Associated with new possibilities, hope, and planting the seeds of future endeavors. Also for transformation and release.

Moon phases, waning crescent: Symbolizes surrender and rest. It is a suitable time for restorative magic, banishing unwanted influences, and tying up loose ends before the start of a new lunar cycle.

Moon phases, waning gibbous: A time for letting go of negative influences, breaking bad habits, and shedding what no longer serves.

Moon phases, waxing crescent: Linked to growth, creativity, and manifestation. Conducive to attracting positive energy, nurturing ideas, and building momentum.

Moon phases, waxing gibbous: A powerful time for refining goals, honing skills, and fine-tuning plans.

Moon water: Water charged with the energy of the moon, often used in rituals, spellwork, and cleansing practices.

Potion: A magical or herbal concoction created for a specific purpose, often consumed or used topically.

Recharging: The process of renewing the energy of magical tools, crystals, or other items that have been utilized in spellwork or rituals. This involves exposing the object to natural elements, such as moonlight, sunlight, or other elements like earth or water, to restore and enhance its magical potency.

Renaissance era (14th to 17th centuries): A historical period marked by a revival of interest in classical art, literature, and philosophy. Visionaries like Agrippa and Dee sought to reconcile magic with emerging scientific thought.

Sabbat: Wiccan festivals that celebrate the changing seasons and agricultural cycles, such as Samhain, Beltane, and Lammas.

Scrying: A divination practice that involves gazing into a reflective surface, such as a crystal ball or water, to receive insights or visions.

Sigil: A unique symbol or design created to encapsulate a specific magical intention, desire, or concept through the transformation of words or phrases.

Solitary Witch: A witch who practices alone rather than within a coven, often developing their own rituals and magical practices.

Sumerian (ca. 4500–1900 B.C.E.): An ancient civilization in

Mesopotamia, known for its contributions to early writing, religious practices, and mythology.

Traditional Witchcraft: A diverse practice that often involves folk magic, ancestral connections, and working with traditional rituals and symbols.

Tool, athame: A ceremonial dagger, often with a double-edged blade, used in rituals and spellwork. It is a symbol of the element of air and is associated with directing energy.

Tool, besom: A ritual broomstick, often used in witchcraft for cleansing spaces, sweeping away negative energies, and symbolizing the union of masculine and feminine energies.

Tool, Book of Shadows: A personal grimoire or journal kept by witches to document their magical practices, spells, rituals, and experiences.

Tool, grimoire: A book of magical knowledge containing spells, rituals, correspondences, and other information related to witchcraft and the occult. *(See also: Book of Shadows.)*

Tool, oracle cards: A divination tool featuring cards with images and messages, providing guidance and insights into various aspects of life.

Tool, runes: Runic symbols and alphabets used for gaining insights, guidance, and answers to questions about the past, present, or future. Rune divination involves casting or drawing runes and interpreting their meanings.

Tool, tarot cards: A deck of 78 cards divided into the Major Arcana (22 cards) and Minor Arcana (56 cards). Tarot cards are used for divination and self-reflection, and as a tool for exploring spiritual and psychological insights. Each card holds symbolic imagery and meanings, offering a method for gaining guidance and understanding.

Victorian era (19th century): A historical period marked by a resurgence of interest in the occult and mysticism. The Victorian era saw a growth in the popularity of spiritualism and the development of esoteric traditions.

Wheel of the Year: A pagan and Wiccan concept representing the annual cycle of seasonal festivals, including Sabbats and solstices.

Wicca: A modern pagan religious movement that involves the worship of nature, the practice of magic, and the veneration of a God and Goddess.

Books by Delia Raven Black

Unleashing Your Inner Witch: An Introductory Guide for New Witches

More Coming Soon!

References

Adler, M. (2014). *Drawing down the moon: Witches, druids, goddess-worshippers, and other pagans in America.* Penguin Books.

Astorino, D. M. (2023, June 28). *12 healing crystals and how to use them.* HowStuffWorks. https://science.howstuffworks.com/environmental/earth/geology/healing-crystals.htm

Astrid The Psychic Witch. (n.d.). *the power of the four elements in witchcraft: Earth, air, fire and water.* Magick & Witchcraft. https://www.magickandwitchcraft.com/post/four-elements-in-witchcraft

The astrology of herbs. (2022, September 29). Anima Mundi Apothecary. https://animamundiherbals.com/blogs/blog/the-astrology-of-herbs

Benedict, P. (1989). [Review of *Servants of Satan: The Age of the Witch Hunts; The Witch-Hunt in Early Modern Europe*, by J. Klaits & B. P. Levack]. *The Journal of Modern History, 61*(3), 571–573. http://www.jstor.org/stable/1881361

Beyer, C. (2018, August 13). *What is chaos magic?* Learn Religions. https://www.learnreligions.com/chaos-magic-95940

Blumberg, J. (2022, October 24). *A brief history of the Salem witch trials.* Smithsonian Magazine. https://www.smithsonianmag.com/history/a-brief-history-of-the-salem-witch-trials-175162489/

Brakels, B. (2023a, October 5). *What is a hedge witch?* Tragic Beautiful. https://www.tragicbeautiful.com/blogs/book-of-spells/what-is-a-hedge-witch

Brakels, B. (2023b, October 5). *What is a kitchen witch?* Tragic Beautiful. https://www.tragicbeautiful.com/blogs/book-of-spells/what-is-a-kitchen-witch

Brigden, J. (n.d.). *The wheel of the year: The calendar of pagan festivals explained.* Sky History. https://www.history.co.uk/articles/the-wheel-of-the-year-the-calendar-of-pagan-festivals-explained

Chamberlain, L. (2023). *Everything you need to know about Wicca!* Wicca Living. https://wiccaliving.com/beginners-guide-wicca-magic/

Chaos magic. (2024, March 5). In *Wikipedia.* https://en.wikipedia.org/w/index.php?title=Chaos_magic&oldid=1211872516

Ciccone, C. (2018, October 31). *Kitchen witchery and simple spells from my Italian grandmothers.* Bon Appétit. https://www.bonappetit.com/story/simple-spells-from-nonnas-kitchen

Cosmic Charlies. (2023, March 15). *"The fascinating history of witchcraft:*

From ancient times to modern day." Medium. https://medium.com/@cosmiccharlies/the-fascinating-history-of-witchcraft-from-ancient-times-to-modern-day-36d331d420c0

Claudat, D. (2022, November 16). *10 sacred herbs that can clear your home of negative energy.* mindbodygreen. https://www.mindbodygreen.com/articles/herbs-to-clear-negative-energy

Clulee, N. H. (2010). At the crossroads of magic and science: John Dee's Archemastrie. In B. Vickers (Ed.), *Occult and scientific mentalities in the Renaissance.* Cambridge University Press, pp. 57–72. https://doi.org/10.1017/cbo9780511572999.003

Crystal meanings. (n.d.). Crystal Earth Spirit. https://crystalearthspirit.com/pages/crystal-meanings

Crystals and their meanings. New Moon Beginnings. https://newmoonbeginnings.com/crystal-meanings/

Crystals meanings. (n.d.). Energy Muse. https://energymuse.com/pages/about-gemstones

Duncan, F. (n.d.). *What is eclectic witchcraft?* The Magickal Path. https://themagickalpath.com/2022/02/01/what-is-eclectic-witchcraft/

Van der Hoeven, J. (2022, October 31). *How I became a hedge witch.* Llewellyn. https://www.llewellyn.com/journal/article/3049

Editorial Team. (2023, November 22). *How to create a witch's garden to import magic into your life!* Balcony Garden Web. https://balconygardenweb.com/how-to-create-a-witchs-garden/

Estrada, J. (2023, July 7). *Why people think cinnamon will bring abundance when sprinkled near your front door.* Well and Good. https://www.wellandgood.com/cinnamon-abundance/

From new moon to full moon: Women's journeys through life. (2023, February 13). Ananda Hum. https://anandahum.com/blogs/yoga/from-new-moon-to-full-moon-womens-journeys-through-life

Greenwood, I. (2023, October 24). *What is chaos magic? A guide to the radical occult practice.* Dazed. https://www.dazeddigital.com/beauty/article/61174/1/what-is-chaos-magick-a-guide-to-the-radical-occult-practice

Hare, J. B. (2004, June 11). Annotated version of Hall, M. *The secret teachings of all ages.* (Original work published 1928). https://www.cia.gov/library/abbottabad-compound/E4/E4AAFF6DAF6863F459A8B4E52DFB9FF4_Manly.P.Hall_The.Secret.Teachings.of.All.Ages.pdf

Hine, P. (2012, July 13). *Condensed Chaos: An Introduction to Chaos Magic.* The Original Falcon Press, p.

The history of green witchcraft. (2020, June 7). Letters to Lilith. https://www.letterstolilith.com/blog/the-history-of-green-witchcraft

History.com Editors. (2023, September 29). *Salem witch trials.* History. https://www.history.com/topics/colonial-america/salem-witch-trials

Johnstone, M. (2006). *The ultimate encyclopedia of spells.* Gramercy Books. https://dl.icdst.org/pdfs/files/105fe4db1927d09e997a5dd03d272122.pdf

Lemke, R. (n.d.). *Four rituals to embody your elemental power*. Earth Speak. https://www.earthspeak.love/earth-speak-blog/rituals-to-embody-elemental-power

Lewis, I. M., & Russell, J. B. (2024, March 19). Witchcraft. In *Encyclopædia Britannica*. Retrieved 26 February 2024 from https://www.britannica.com/topic/witchcraft

Lyons, S. (n.d.). *An introduction to chaos magic: Exclusive excerpt from How to Study Magic*. Hachette Book Group. https://www.rpmystic.com/excerpts/an-introduction-to-chaos-magic-exclusive-excerpt-from-how-to-study-magic-a-guide-to-history-lore-and-building-your-own-practice/

Machlab, I. (n.d.). *Magic properties of plants then and now*. Natufia Smart Garden. https://natufia.com/magic-properties-of-plants-then-and-now/

Madara, M. (2017, September 8). *A Spellbinding guide to cooking like a witch*. Vice. https://www.vice.com/en/article/vvqbnb/a-spellbinding-guide-to-cooking-like-a-witch

Martinez, N. (2024, February 20). *Ask a witch: Protection spells for beginners*. Nylon. https://www.nylon.com/life/how-to-use-protection-spells-rituals-magic

March, B. (2024, January 3). *A beginner's guide to using crystals*. Harper's Bazaar. https://www.harpersbazaar.com/uk/beauty/fitness-wellbeing/a43244/crystal-healing-beginners-guide/

Netzer, J. (2020, August 25). *What is a green witch? The beginner's guide to embracing earthly magick*. Cratejoy. https://www.cratejoy.com/box-insider/green-witch-primer/

Pie the Wonder. (2023, November 15). *3 signs you're a chaos witch*.

Medium. https://medium.com/@piethewonder/3-signs-youre-a-chaos-witch-b3fc6ddac4aa

Pretty Spirits. (2023, July 6). *Using aromatherapy for spiritual healing.* https://prettyspirits.com/blogs/blog/balancing-energies-through-scents-aromatherapy-spiritual-healing

Rampling, J. M. (2012). John Dee and the sciences: Early modern networks of knowledge. *Studies in History and Philosophy of Science Part A, 43*(3), 432–436. https://doi.org/10.1016/j.shpsa.2011.12.001

Rekstis, E. (2023, November 14). *Healing crystals 101: Everything you need to know.* Healthline. https://www.healthline.com/health/mental-health/guide-to-healing-crystals

Rose, M. (2024, January 25). *Full moon rituals & spells: 8 easy ways to harness the magic & use it to your benefit.* StyleCaster. https://stylecaster.com/lifestyle/zodiac/1017776/full-moon-rituals/

Sack, H. (2019, July 13). *John Dee and his world of science and magic.* SciHi Blog. http://scihi.org/john-dee/

6 easy to grow herbs in your kitchen garden. (2024, January 23). WhatToGrow. https://www.whattogrow.co.uk/6-herbs-easy-to-grow-in-your-kitchen-garden/

Szaro, M. (2023). *Botanical Archives.* Herbal Academy. https://theherbalacademy.com/blog/herbs-for-health-and-cheer/

Szonyi, G. E. (2010). *John Dee's Occultism.* State University of New York Press.

Three Books of Occult Philosophy. (2023, May 23). In *Wikipedia*. https://en.wikipedia.org/w/index.php?title=Three_Books_of_Occult_Philosophy&oldid=1156527593

Vitimus, A. (2009, January 12). *Chaos magic: The misunderstood path*. Llewellyn. https://www.llewellyn.com/journal/article/1799

Wallenfeldt, J. (n.d.). Salem witch trials. In *Encyclopædia Britannica*. Retrieved February 26, 2024 from https://www.britannica.com/event/Salem-witch-trials.

Ward, K. (2022, August 6). *FYI: There are many types of witches*. Cosmopolitan. https://www.cosmopolitan.com/lifestyle/a37681530/types-of-witches/

What is a hedge witch? (n.d.). Mabon House. https://www.mabonhouse.co/new-blog/what-is-a-hedge-witch

The wheel of the year: Understanding the 8 seasonal festivals. (2023, May 15). Bloom and Manifest. https://www.bloomandmanifest.com/wheel-of-the-year/

White, E. D. (2024, March 5). Wicca. In *Encyclopædia Britannica*. Retrieved February 26, 2024 from https://www.britannica.com/topic/Wicca.

Wicca Down Under. (2023, November 29). *Herbs in Wicca* [Video]. YouTube. https://www.youtube.com/watch?v=scnEmyqVu84

Wigington, P. (2019a, June 25). *How to create a sacred space for pagan rituals*. Learn Religions. https://www.learnreligions.com/how-to-create-sacred-space-2561781

Wigington, P. (2019b, August 19). *What Is a hedge witch? Practices and beliefs.* Learn Religions. https://www.learnreligions.com/hedge-witch-4768392

Wolfe, S. E. (n.d.). *How to write your own witchcraft spells.* Green Witch Living. https://blog.greenwitchliving.com/writing-your-own-witchcraft-spells/

Zucker, S., & Harris, B. (n.d.). *A beginner's guide to the Age of Enlightenment.* Khan Academy. https://www.khanacademy.org/humanities/renaissance-reformation/rococo-neoclassicism/rococo/a/a-beginners-guide-to-the-age-of-enlightenment

Image References

All images provided by the author.

Witchy Products

I know it can be overwhelming when you first dip your feet into the world of witchcraft, and my goal is to help the getting started process be smooth and easy, which includes helping you get the supplies you'll need to get going!

Thus, I've compiled a list of Witchy Product Recommendations for you – everything from whole witch starter kits to herbs to candles to wands – which I have put on my website for you so that I can keep these recommendations as up-to-date as possible for you.

I invite you to go to the following link to access your Witchy Product Recommendations:

https://www.unleashingyourinnerwitch.com/post/witchy-product-recommendations

Or Scan the QR Code on the Following Page:

Delia Raven Black

About the Author

Delia Raven Black, a passionate and experienced practitioner of witchcraft, is thrilled to present her debut work as an author, *Unleashing Your Inner Witch: An Introductory Guide for New Witches*. Delia's enchantment with witchcraft began during a childhood visit to Salem, Massachusetts, igniting a lifelong journey to explore and uncover its mysteries. With a keen interest in guiding budding witches, Delia aims to demystify witchcraft for novices through this and future writings, fostering the untapped magical potential that she believes rests inside every human being.

Delia resides in a cozy New England cabin with her husband, Matthew, and their Siamese cat, Moonlight.

Printed in Great Britain
by Amazon

43385877R00096